The Little OXEN

Programme Booklet

WALTER FIRTH

BALBOA.
PRESS

A DIVISION OF HAY HOUSE

Vetus Testamentum Graece, Secundum Septuaginta Interpretes, Nova Impressio, Lipsiae, 1868

The Greek New Testament, Deutsche Bibelgesellschaft, Stuttgart, Germany, 2007

Balboa Press books may be ordered through booksellers or by contacting:

Balboa Press
A Division of Hay House
1663 Liberty Drive
Bloomington, IN 47403
www.balboapress.com.au
1 (877) 407-4847

ISBN: 978-1-5043-0910-3 (sc)
ISBN: 978-1-5043-0911-0 (e)

Print information available on the last page.

Balboa Press rev. date: 07/19/2017

Contents

Right from Wrong

Consequences of Doing Things We Shouldn't...1

Jealousy...4

Pride and Vanity...6

Self-Centred Greed or Envy..8

The Greed of Hoarding...10

Saying Wrong Things...12

Being Thankful and Forgiving and Not Ungrateful...14

Character

Character: Luke 10:25-28...19

Home/kingdom: Psalm 84:1-4 & Genesis 1:1-3...21

Ability: Acts of the Apostles 27:27-40...23

Respect: 1 Peter 2:9-17..25

Acceptance: Luke19:1-10...26

Caring: Luke 15:3-7...27

Trust: Proverbs. 3:5 & Exodus 14:19-30...29

Emotion: Ecclesiastes 3:1-8...33

Royalty: Matthew 22:11...35

Character: 37

Living A Fruitful Life

Perseverance Hebrews 12:1-11 41

Don't Be Lazy Proverbs 6:6-8 / Proverbs 26:13-17...43

Right Priorities Mark 10:17-31 44

Don't Waste Your Talent 1 Corinthians 12:4-31 46

Heavenly Treasures Matthew 13:44-49 48

Count Your Blessings Job 37:14-19 50

Be a Good Example Luke 10:25-37 52

Walk the Narrow Path Matthew 7:13 55

Success

Self Control Genesis 26:17-22..59

Stillness 1 Kings 19: 1-13 60

Learning Patience Genesis 17:1-6, 17 63

Willpower Matthew 4:1-11 66

Bravery Ezra, chapters 7-8 69

Success/Achieving Goals..71

Humility Luke18:10-14 75

Forgiveness Luke 15:11-32 76

Sharing John 6:1–13...78

Communal Living

Helping and healing John 5:1-15 83

Inclusion 1 Corinthians 12:12-27 85

Responsibility Ezekiel 33:1-19...87

Anxiety Matthew 6:25-34 89

Resting Matthew 11:28-30 91

Seeing the bigger picture 1 Corinthians 13:10-13 92

Judging Others Matthew 7:1-5 and Romans 12:16-19.....................93

Fruits of the Spirit

Fruits of the Spirit Galatians 5:22-23 97

Love 98

Joy...99

Peace 99

Patience...101

Kindness 103

Goodness 103

Faithfulness..104

Gentleness 108

Self-control..111

Being Kind

Acts of Kindness Luke 5:17-26 115

Love your Enemies Luke 6:27-36 117

Showing Kindness Luke 10:25-37 119

Responding to Kindness 1 Samuel 25:2-42 and Psalm 94:1-2. 122

Jesus is kind to Children Mark 10:13-16. 126

Be kind to All Numbers 22:21-39..127

Generosity

Jesus feeds the 5000 Mark 6:34-44 134

Elijah and the Widow at Zarephath 1 Kings 17:7-16.....................136

Elisha and the Shunammite couple II Kings 4:8-10 138

Dorcas (Tabitha) Acts of the Apostles 9:36-42 141

The Whole Armour of God

Ephesians 6:10-20 145

Helmet Of Salvation 146

Sword Of The Spirit 151

Shield Of Faith 153

Breastplate Of Righteousness 156

Belt Of Truth 160

Sandals Of Peace 163

ABC through the Bible

A. Acts of the Apostles 168

B. Book of Baruch 170

C. 2 Chronicles 172

D. Daniel 174

E. Esther 177

G. Genesis 181

H. Habakkuk 183

I. Isaiah 186

J. Judith 190

K. Kings 193

L. Luke 195

M. Maccabees 197

N. Nehemiah 199

O. Obadiah 201

P. Peter 204

R. Ruth 206

S. Sirach 208

T. Tobit 210

W. Wisdom 212

Z. The Book of Zechariah 214

When I first began ministry, I realised that whilst there was an effort being put into children's ministries, nearly every programme that was being implemented was a purchased programme from overseas. However, these programmes have not been tested, adapted, or designed for our current Australian culture where 61 per cent of people identify as Christian; yet less than a quarter of Christians attending church weekly.

Often our communities- that is, the ones outside of our churches- are made up of a spread of backgrounds, educational achievement and social systems.

In an effort to reach and build up spiritually cognitive children with a healthy sense of self and a positive ethical and moral framework to guide their lives, we set out to create a programme built on a series of themed lessons grounded in the Scriptures. They were designed to cater to a wide range of skills, capabilities and education regardless of family or socio-economic backgrounds.

Some of the lessons come with an actual craft to be constructed with the lesson. Some lessons however, require basic materials as the craft is created from scratch. Most of the craft included in these lessons come at minimal cost in order to enable more churches and community groups to feel confident in running children's programmes, regardless of funding. As these lessons are designed to show, model and integrate better ways of being to the children, sequential lessons throughout each series will cover the same points for reinforcement.

Whilst we are ever grateful for the volunteers who give so much for the Church and her mission, I am aware that not every congregation has the numbers of volunteers needed for many of the programmes on the market. As such, Little Oxen has been designed to run with a minimum of two people, with at least one being a leader.

These lessons normally take 2 hours. Please keep in mind this lesson structure is not compulsory. It is a starting point from which you can adapt this structure to fit your own community and setting.

Start with a time of sharing. Encourage each child to share something about the week - be it a good thing or a bad thing. Listen carefully and stay with them in what they are saying. Close this section with a prayer.

Move over to where afternoon tea is provided. Have them sit and eat. After this is a good time for a toilet break.

When children are ready, sit them down and do the talk and reading for the day, with a little discussion afterwards. Explain the craft, and have them move over to preset table to do activity.

When they are finished, give them some free time to run around and play.

You may want to close in a prayer, but I have found that the nature of pick up means this rarely happens smoothly.

Right from Wrong

This is a series of lessons that work off the principle that we are all usually doing the right thing, but that when we do the wrong thing, our actions produce a set of consequences that either diminish who we are as people or have a profound effect on those around us.

Consequences of Doing Things We Shouldn't

This lesson uses the story of Adam and Eve to draw attention to the fact our actions have consequences and that, when we do the wrong thing, the consequences can be severe. As you tell the story, try to draw out what they should have done, and link it into children's everyday lives by asking if they have 'ever been told not to touch something and have', following up with a question about what happened.

Adam and Eve: Genesis 2:4-14, 2:15-21

When God made the earth and the heavens, God made a man from the ground, and breathed the breath of life into his nostrils. The man then became a living being.

God planted a garden in Eden. There he put the man. God made all kinds of trees grow out of the ground—trees that were pleasing to the eye and good for food. In the middle of the garden were the tree of life and the tree of the knowledge of good and evil.

God put the man in the Garden of Eden to work it and take care of it. God told the man, "You are free to eat from any tree in the garden; but you must not eat from the tree of the knowledge of good and evil, for when you eat from it you will certainly die."

God said, "It is not good for the man to be alone. I will make a helper suitable for him."

God caused the man to fall into a deep sleep; and while he was sleeping, he took one of the man's ribs and then made a woman from the rib, and God brought her to the man.

Now the serpent was more crafty than any of the wild animals God had made. He said to the woman, "Did God really say, 'You must not eat from any tree in the garden'?"

The woman said to the serpent, "We may eat fruit from the trees in the garden, but God did say, 'You must not eat fruit from the tree that is in the middle of the garden, and you must not touch it, or you will die.'"

"You will not certainly die," the serpent said to the woman. "For God knows that when you eat from it your eyes will be opened, and you will be like God, knowing good and evil."

When the woman saw that the fruit of the tree was good for food and pleasing to the eye, and also desirable for gaining wisdom, she took some and ate it. She also gave some to Adam, who was with her, and he ate it. Then the eyes of both of them were opened, and they realized they were naked; so they sewed fig leaves together and made coverings for themselves.

Then the man and his wife heard the sound of God as he was walking in the garden in the cool of the day, and they hid from the Lord God among the trees of the garden. But the Lord God called to the man, "Where are you?"

He answered, "I heard you in the garden, and I was afraid because I was naked; so I hid."

And he said, "Who told you that you were naked? Have you eaten from the tree that I commanded you not to eat from?"

The man said, "The woman you put here with me—she gave me some fruit from the tree, and I ate it."

Then the Lord God said to the woman, "What is this you have done?"

The woman said, "The serpent deceived me, and I ate."

So the Lord God said to the serpent, "Because you have done this, "Cursed are you above all livestock and all wild animals! You will crawl on your belly and you will eat dust all the days of your life. And I will put enmity between you and the woman, and between your offspring and hers; he will crush your head, and you will strike his heel."

To the woman he said,

"I will make your pains in childbearing very severe; with painful labour you will give birth to children. Your desire will be for your husband, and he will rule over you."

To Adam he said, "Because you listened to your wife and ate fruit from the tree about which I commanded you, 'You must not eat from it,'

"Cursed is the ground because of you; through painful toil you will eat food from it all the days of your life. It will produce thorns and thistles for you, and you will eat the plants of the field. By the sweat of your brow you will eat your food until you return to the ground, since from it you were taken; for dust you are and to dust you will return."

Craft Activity: Serpent in the Garden-

Get children to colour in the worksheet. Children then cut out the picture, and cut on the dotted line on the tree and pock the serpent through from the back of the page. Fold along the fold marks to create the scene.

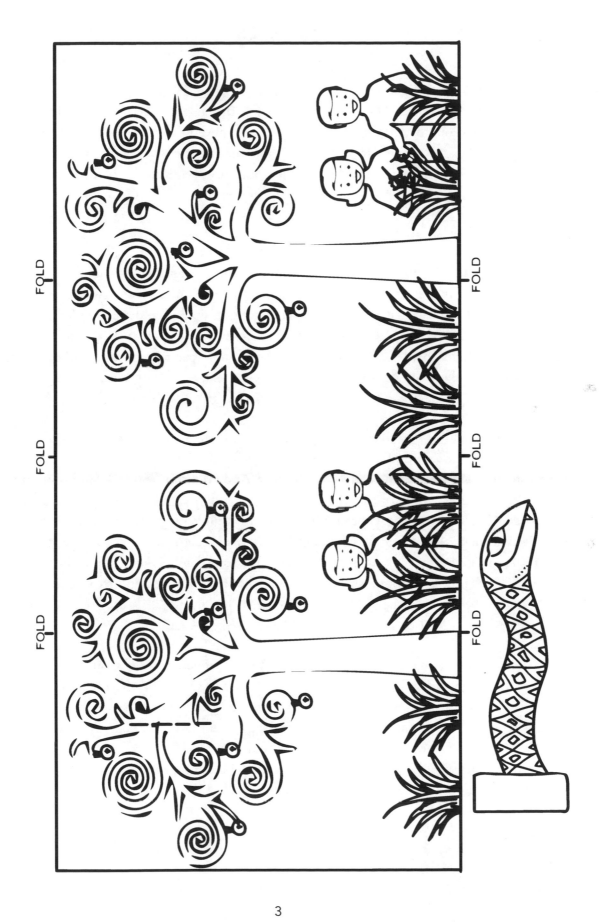

Jealousy

This lesson uses the story of the murder of Abel to try to show not only the nastiness of jealousy, but also the progression that takes place in our thoughts and hearts long before we act physically. It is important to draw this out as you discuss the story and craft because our thoughts and the way we play them out can be just as wrong as if we had actually stabbed someone, as in the old saying; 'staring daggers at someone'.

Cain and Abel: Genesis 4:1-10

Adam and Eve had their first baby. They named him Cain. Then they had another, Cain's little brother, and they named him Abel. When Cain got older he became a farmer. When Abel grew up he became a shepherd. One day Cain and Abel brought gifts to God to thank him for all the good things he had done for them. Cain brought some of the things he had grown. Abel brought the first lamb born to one of his sheep. God was happy with Abel's gift, because he saw that Abel really wanted to please God and always do what God wanted. But God knew that Cain wasn't so sure he wanted to do what God wanted. So God wasn't happy with Cain's gift and that made Cain mad.

God loved Cain, and he said to him, "Why are you scowling? If you always do what is right, you will be happy. But be careful. Bad thoughts will ruin your life. Learn to control them." But Cain didn't listen to God. Instead he blamed his brother. And even though God loved both brothers as much as anyone could ever be loved, Cain thought God loved Abel more than him. So from that day on, Cain began to think mean things about his younger brother. He kept thinking them and thinking them. And the more he thought them, the harder it was to stop. And the more he thought them, the meaner his thoughts became. Until one day he planned a terrible thing! He said to his brother; "Abel, come with me out into the fields." Abel went because he loved and trusted his brother. And so they walked out into the fields. And when Cain got Abel out where nobody could see or hear them, he took a rock and he killed Abel.

Later God found Cain out working and asked; "Where is Abel?" "How should I know?" Cain replied. "Am I supposed to take care of my brother?" But God knew the terrible thing Cain had done. God said to him, "I see your brother's blood on the ground! Because you have spilled your brother's blood into the ground, the ground won't grow your crops for you anymore. From now on you will have to wander in far away places to find your food." "Lord, the punishment is too hard for me!" Cain said. "My relatives will try to kill me when they hear what I have done. I will always be running." So God put a mark on Cain to protect him.

Then on a sad, sad day, Cain left his only home and family. Because of the evil thing Cain had done, Adam and Eve lost not just one son, but two. Cain lost his family. Cain went away and lived in the land of Nod.

Craft Activity: The Little Paper Daggers-

Daggers hurt and kill. If we are not careful, being angry and jealous can lead us to hurt people, even if we do not mean to. And if we let this sort of behaviour rule our lives, the consequences can be terrible. Children get a handout of the craft, colour and cut out.

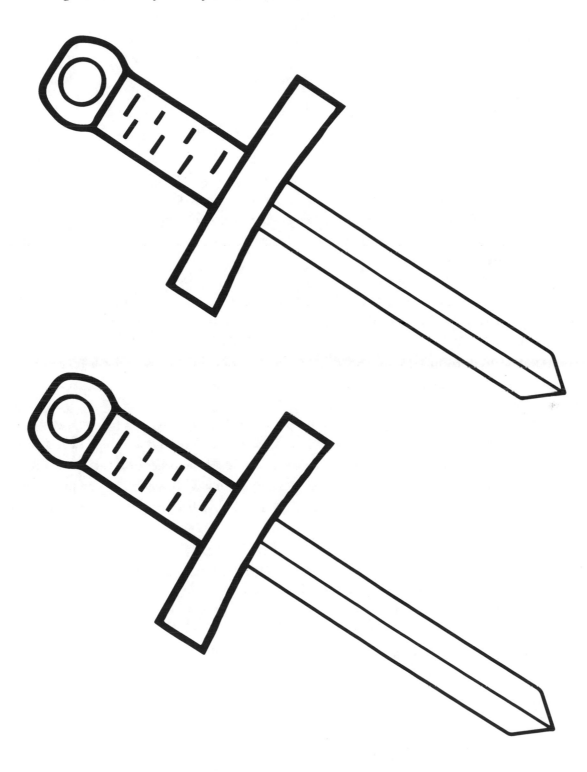

Pride and Vanity

Whilst pride does have positive aspects, its danger is that it can become quite inflated with its negative shadow side. The negative version of pride is considered the original and most serious of the seven deadly sins - the perversion of the faculties that make humans more like God- dignity and holiness. It is also thought to be the source of the other capital sins. It is identified as dangerously corrupt selfishness, the putting of one's own desires, urges, wants, and whims before the welfare of other people.

Uzziah, King of Judah: 2 Chronicles 26: 1-21

Uzziah was sixteen years old when he became king, and he reigned in Jerusalem for fifty-two years. He sought God during the days of Zechariah, who instructed him in the fear of God. As long as he sought the Lord, God gave him success. He went to war against the Philistines and broke down the walls of Gath, Jabneh and Ashdod. He then rebuilt towns near Ashdod and elsewhere among the Philistines.

But after Uzziah became powerful, his pride led to his downfall. He was unfaithful to God, and entered the temple of God to burn incense on the altar of incense. Azariah the priest with eighty other courageous priests followed him in. They confronted King Uzziah and said, "It is not right for you, Uzziah, to burn incense to God. That is for the priests, who have been consecrated to burn incense. Leave the sanctuary, for you have been unfaithful."

Uzziah, who had a censer in his hand ready to burn incense, became angry. While he was raging at the priests in the Lord's temple, the hot coals and incense fell out and a terrible skin disease broke out on his forehead. When Azariah the chief priest and all the other priests looked at him, they saw the terrible skin disease, so they hurried him out. Uzziah was eager to leave. King Uzziah had this terrible skin disease until the day he died. He had to live in a separate building and was banned from the temple.

Uzziah started off nice. But his fame, success and fortune started to make him change. He became arrogant and full of pride. He made a big mistake and did the wrong thing when he entered the temple and offered incense upon the altar. The priests tried to stop him. Pride got in the way. He ended up getting a terrible skin disease. This is like when we are told by someone not to go somewhere or not to do something, and we do it anyway. Maybe we've been told not to play on the road or run across the road. If we do then we might get hurt badly.

Craft Activity: X-ray of Hand-

This craft is to remind children that if we do the wrong thing or go places we should not we may end up getting hurt. To do this craft, get a piece of black card, some white paint and some chalk. Cut each piece of black card to A3 size, and paint each child's hand with white paint. Get them to press their hands carefully and firmly onto the card. Use a paintbrush to paint onto their hand; this will keep the paint thin, allow it to dry quickly, and create an x-ray like appearance. Then, after having let it sit for a few minutes, use the chalk to draw little dashes or trace bone outlines into the white paint.

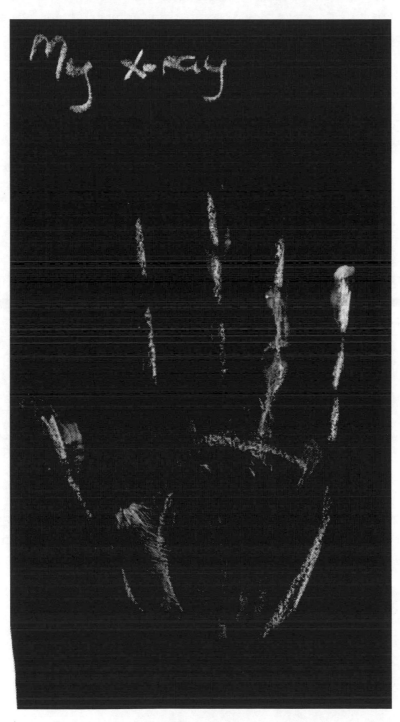

Self-Centred Greed or Envy

Greed, also known as avarice or covetousness, is a sin of desire. However, greed (as seen by the Church) tends to be more narrowly applied to an artificial, rapacious desire and pursuit of material possessions. Thomas Aquinas wrote, "Greed is a sin against God, just as all mortal sins, in as much as man condemns things eternal for the sake of temporal things." Hoarding of materials or objects, theft and robbery- especially by means of violence, trickery, or manipulation of authority- are all actions that may be inspired by greed.

The Parable of the Workers in the Vineyard: Matthew 20:1-16

The kingdom of heaven is like a landowner who went out early in the morning to hire workers for his vineyard. He agreed to pay them a proper day's wage for the day and sent them into his vineyard.

"About nine in the morning he went out and saw others standing in the marketplace where people waited to find work doing nothing. He told them, 'You also go and work in my vineyard, and I will pay you whatever is right.' So they went.

"He went out again about noon and about three in the afternoon and did the same thing. About five in the afternoon he went out and found still others standing around. He asked them, 'Why have you been standing here all day long doing nothing?'

"'Because no one has hired us,' they answered.

"He said to them, 'You also go and work in my vineyard.'

"When evening came, the owner of the vineyard said to his foreman, 'Call the workers and pay them their wages, beginning with the last ones hired and going on to the first.'

"The workers who were hired about five in the afternoon came and each received a proper day's wage. So when those came who were hired first, they expected to receive more. But each one of them also received a denarius. When they received it, they began to grumble against the landowner. 'These who were hired last worked only one hour,' they said, 'and you have made them equal to us who have borne the burden of the work and the heat of the day.'

"But he answered one of them, 'I am not being unfair to you, friend. Didn't you agree to work for a proper day's wage? Take your pay and go. I want to give the one who was hired last the same as I gave you. Don't I have the right to do what I want with my own money? Or are you envious because I am generous?'

Craft Activity: Tools-

When we are working at something we need to be pleased with what we do and get and not be envious or greedy about what others around us are getting.

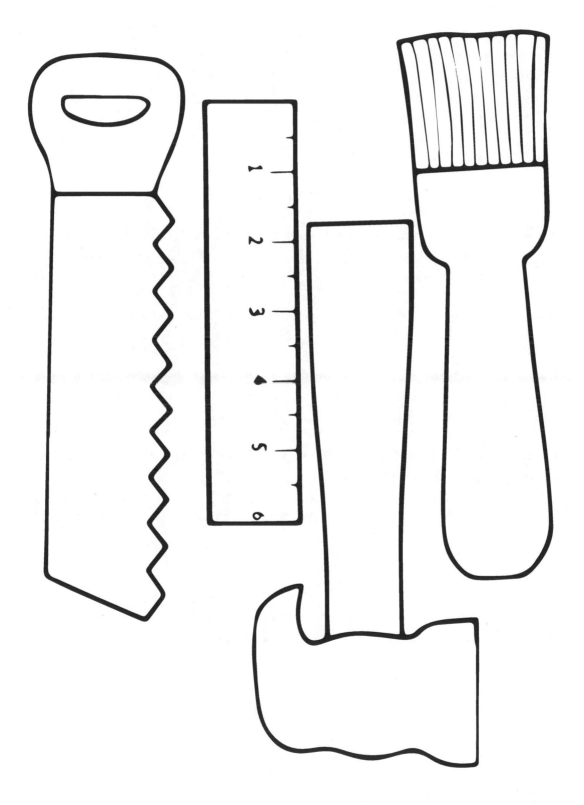

The Greed of Hoarding

A **hoard** or 'wealth deposit' is a collection of valuable objects, sometimes purposely buried in the ground. This would usually be with the intention of later recovery by the hoarder; hoarders sometimes died before retrieving the hoard, and these surviving hoards may be uncovered much later by other people. Like the lesson on *self-centred greed or envy*, this lesson focuses on another aspect of greed that sees people waste, time, relationships and sometimes their lives building up investments that give no deeper value.

The Parable of the Rich Fool: Luke 12:13-21

Someone in the crowd said to Jesus, "Teacher, tell my brother to divide the inheritance with me."

Jesus replied, "Who appointed me a judge or an arbiter between you?" Then he said to them, "Watch out! Be on your guard against all kinds of greed; life does not consist in an abundance of possessions. Life is not about the things you own!"

And Jesus told them this parable: "The ground of a certain rich man yielded an abundant harvest. He thought to himself, 'What shall I do? I have no place to store my crops.'

"Then he said, 'This is what I'll do. I will tear down my barns and build bigger ones, and there I will store my surplus grain. And I'll say to myself, "You have plenty of grain laid up for many years. Take life easy; eat, drink and be merry."'

"But God said to him, 'You fool! This very night your life will be demanded from you. Then who will get what you have prepared for yourself?'

"This is how it will be with whoever stores up things for themselves but is not rich toward God."

Craft activity: The Barn-

If we spend all our time trying to have more and more things or do bigger and bigger things, or if we spend our time trying to make more and more money, then we will end up never having the time to enjoy what we have or the people we have in life around us. Children need to colour and cut out their barn. They will need to fold along the dotted lined and glue the tabs.

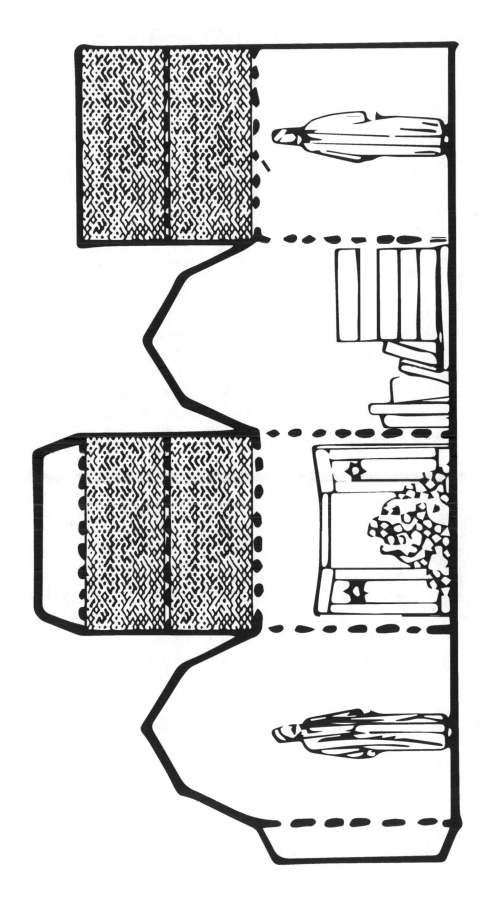

Saying Wrong Things

It is not just what we do that is right or wrong. Our words have the ability to do wrongs far greater at times than our ability to do physical wrongs. This lesson is a reminder of this type of wrongdoing, along with the reverse: that we can instead use our speech to praise and lift up others.

Controlling what we say is hard: it is wrong to say mean things or lies or stories about others. It is hard to only say nice things or not say mean things, but if you work at it, it will be easier to behave in other areas too.

What We Say: James 3:2-12

Dear brothers and sisters, not many of you should become teachers in the church, for we who teach will be judged more strictly. Indeed, we all make many mistakes. For if we could control our tongues, we would be perfect and would then be able to also control ourselves in every other way.

We can make a large horse go wherever we want by means of a small bit in its mouth. And a small rudder makes a huge ship turn wherever the pilot chooses to go, even though the winds are strong. In the same way, the tongue is a small thing that makes grand speeches.

But a tiny spark can set a great forest on fire. And among all the parts of the body, the tongue is like a flame of fire. It is a whole world of wickedness, corrupting your entire body. It can set your whole life on fire.

People can tame all kinds of animals, birds, reptiles, and fish, but no one can tame the tongue. It can be restless and evil, full of deadly poison. Sometimes it praises our Lord and God, and sometimes it curses those who have been made in the image of God. And so blessing and cursing come pouring out of the same mouth. Surely, my brothers and sisters, this is not right! Does a spring of water bubble out with both fresh water and bitter water? Does a fig tree produce olives, or a grapevine produce figs? No, and you can't draw fresh water from a salty spring. Watch then, what you say so that only nice things come from you.

Craft activity: Frog with Long Tongue-

Fold the frog template on its front shoulders, back hips and ankles to make it 3D. Using a piece of left over paper, cut a long rectangle and roll it up to be the tongue. Stick it to the underside of the head.

Being Thankful and Forgiving and Not Ungrateful

The Parable of the Unmerciful Servant: Matthew 18:21-35

Then Peter came to Jesus and asked; 'Lord, if my brother keeps on hurting me, how many times should I forgive him? Should I forgive him seven times?'

'No, not just seven times, but forgive him seventy times seven times', Jesus replied.

'It is like this story. Once upon a time there was a king who wanted to collect all the money that his servants owed him. So he began to do this. Then they brought a man to him who owed him millions of silver coins. The man was not able to pay. So the king ordered them to sell the man, his wife, his children and all his possessions. The king would receive that money to pay the servant's debt. Then the servant knelt in front of the king; "Be patient with me", he said. "I will pay back everything that I owe you." And the king pitied him. So he forgave the servant for all that he owed. And he let the servant leave free.

That servant went out. But he found one of the other servants who owed him just a few silver coins. The first servant held the second servant firmly. He began to squeeze the second servant's neck. "Pay back what you owe me!" he demanded.

The second servant kneeled down in front of him. "Be patient with me and I will pay you back", he said.

But the first servant refused. Instead, he caused the authorities to throw the other servant into prison. And he had to stay there until he could pay back the debt. The rest of the servants saw what had happened. And they were very upset about it. So they told the king everything that had happened.

Then the king called the first servant to come back to him. "You wicked servant", he said, "I forgave all your debt to me because you asked me to. You should have pitied the other servant, just as I pitied you!" The king was very angry. So he handed the servant over to the prison officers for punishment. He must stay in prison until he paid everything back.

You must forgive your brothers. God who is in heaven will act like this king towards each of you. So you must forgive them from deep inside yourselves.'"

It is important to forgive others as God, parents, and friends forgive us.

Craft activity: Flowers-

People tend to give flowers to others as a sign of caring, a sign of loving. Flowers are also given as a sign to say; 'I'm sorry'.

Step 1

Draw a spiral on any size square of paper (the bigger the square, the bigger the flower).

If you feel confident in your skills, just go ahead and cut out a spiral shape without drawing the spiral from your square of paper.

Step 2

With a pencil or Q-tip, roll the end of the paper towards you until you reach the end of the spiral.

Be sure to keep a tight roll.

Step 3

When you've reached the end, gently pull out the pencil or Q-tip.

You're done!

Character

This is a series of lessons that moves through the letters of the word 'character' to help explain some aspects of what we would term healthy or good.

The first lesson in this series explains what 'character' is, and the last lesson focuses on the children's own individual character.

Character: Luke 10:25-28

character

noun: **character**; plural noun: **characters**

1 1. the mental and moral qualities distinctive to an individual. "running away was not in keeping with her character"

Just then a lawyer stood up to test Jesus. 'Teacher,' he said, 'what must I do to inherit eternal life?' Jesus said to him, 'What is written in the law? What do you read there?' He answered, 'You shall love the Lord your God with all your heart, and with all your soul, and with all your strength, and with all your mind; and your neighbour as yourself.' And he said to him, 'You have given the right answer; do this, and you will live.'

Craft Activity: Heart Craft Tissue by Numbers-

Materials:

1. Heart Template
2. Tissue Paper – Red, Pink, White
3. Black Marker
4. Glue
5. Scissors
6. Dark Red Cardboard

Print out the heart template and add your numbered sections 1, 2, & 3. Assign the colours to a number and scrunch and paste. When the heart is complete stick onto red cardboard and write the names of the people we love or who love us around it.

Home/kingdom: Psalm 84:1-4 & Genesis 1:1-3

This lesson is designed to help children focus on the fact that we are members of God's kingdom, but also that we are called to look over, care for and protect the world around us.

Psalm 84

How lovely is your home and dwelling place,
    God the Almighty!

My soul yearns, even faints,
    for the courts of you my Lord;
my heart and my flesh cry out
    for the living God.

Even the sparrow, such a little bird, has found a home,
    and the swallow a nest for herself,
    where she may have her baby birds—
a place near your altar,
    Lord Almighty, my King and my God.

Blessed are those who dwell in your house;
    they are forever praising you.

Genesis 1:1-3

In the beginning God created the heavens and the earth. Before God made people, the earth was formless and empty, darkness was over the surface of the deep, and the Spirit of God was hovering over the waters.

Our God made all that there is. God saw it when the universe was a raw canvas and created something truly beautiful and amazing. God made this for us, for those who came before us, and for those who will come after us. We should all seek to reach out, care for and be a part of this bigger picture, this great celestial kingdom God has.

Craft Activity: Castle-

Just as a king, Queen Lord or Lady in their castle needed to look after and protect all in their domain, people land and animals, we are called to do the same. Children will need two copies of the castle wall printed on card stock. Children cut them out, fold in half to make right angles, then stick together. They can cut out their own windows or doors if they wound like.

Ability: Acts of the Apostles 27:27-40

ability

noun: **ability** plural noun: **abilities**

a. The quality of being able to do something, especially the physical, mental, financial, or legal power to accomplish something.

b. A skill, talent, or capacity

Whilst it seems there are things each of us are good at, many of our abilities are good because we work on them. Sometimes by practicing, sometimes by training. One aspect (thing) people with healthy characters have is the ability to rise up and do what they need to do in whatever situation they find themselves in.

The Shipwreck

Once, Paul was on a ship. For fourteen nights they were being driven across the Adriatic Sea in terrible conditions. About midnight the sailors sensed they were approaching land. They took soundings and found that the water was about 35 metres deep. A short time later they took soundings again and found it was about 25 metres deep. Fearing that they would be dashed against the rocks, they dropped four anchors from the stern and prayed for daylight. In an attempt to escape from the ship, the sailors let the lifeboat down into the sea, pretending they were going to lower some anchors from the bow. Then Paul said to the centurion and the soldiers, "Unless these men stay with the ship, you cannot be saved." So the soldiers cut the ropes that held the lifeboat and let it drift away.

Just before dawn Paul urged them all to eat. "For the last fourteen days," he said, "you have been in constant suspense and you haven't eaten anything. Now I urge you to take some food. You need it to survive. Not one of you will lose a single hair from his head." After he said this, he took some bread and gave thanks to God in front of them all. Then he broke it and began to eat. They were all encouraged and ate some food themselves. Altogether there were 276 people on board. When they had eaten as much as they wanted, they lightened the ship by throwing the grain into the sea.

When daylight came, they did not recognize the land, but they saw a bay with a sandy beach, where they decided to run the ship aground if they could. Cutting loose the anchors, they left them in the sea and at the same time untied the ropes that held the rudders. Then they hoisted the foresail to the wind and made for the beach. They reached the shore safely and all was well.

Craft Activity: Boat. Print template and cut the outside lines. Fold the inside lines and stick down the black tabs. Push a toothpick through the dots and then add sail to the boat.

Sail

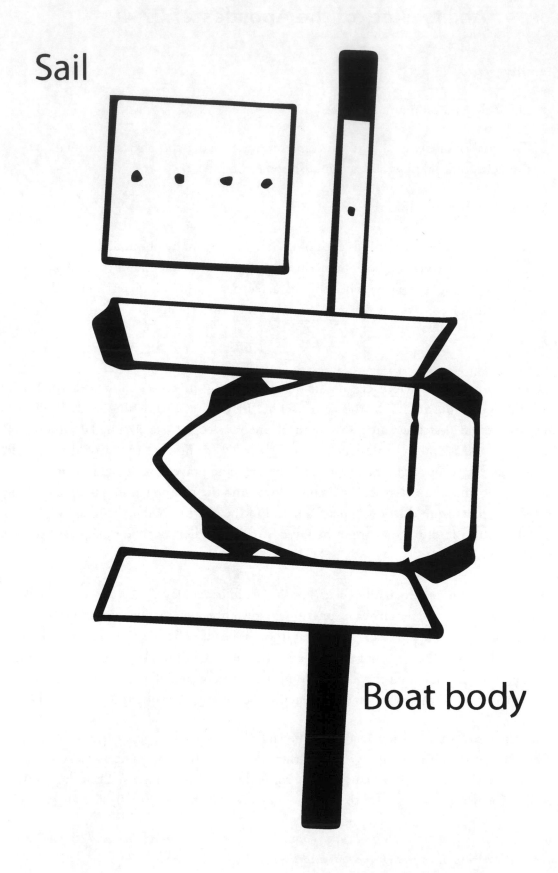

Boat body

Respect: 1 Peter 2:9-17

You are a chosen race, a royal priesthood, a holy nation, God's very own people, in order that you may proclaim the mighty acts of him who called you out of darkness into his marvellous light. And you need to live lives that show this, that you believe it of yourself and of others around you.

Once you were not a people,
but now you are God's people;
once you had not received mercy,
but now you have received mercy.

You are loved and I urge you to conduct yourselves honourably among other people, especially among those who are different to you, so that, though they may malign you as evildoers or say mean things about you, they might see your honourable deeds and the respectful things you do, and glorify God when God comes to judge.

For the Lord's sake accept the authority of every human institution, whether of the emperor as supreme, or of governors, as sent by him to punish those who do wrong and to praise those who do right, or your teachers or your parents who try to teach you the right way of living. For it is God's will that by doing right you should silence the ignorance of the foolish. As servants of God, live as free people, yet do not use your freedom as a pretext for evil. Honour everyone. Love the family of believers. Fear God. Honour the emperor.

Craft Activity: Tree of Good Manners-

Manners are one way of showing respect for others. For this craft, children will need three different coloured pieces of paper: background, 'leaves' & 'tree'. Children trace their hand onto one piece to be the tree. In each finger they write the manners they are all ready good at. They then cut out their 'leaves' paper and stick that to their background followed by their hand tree. Then, 'growing' up and into the hand are the aspects that help grow our manners such as patience, empathy.

Acceptance: Luke19:1-10

Jesus and Zacchaeus

Jesus entered Jericho and was passing through it. A man was there named Zacchaeus; he was a chief tax-collector and was rich. He was trying to see who Jesus was, but on account of the crowd he could not, because he was very short. So he ran ahead and climbed a sycomore tree to see him, because Jesus was going to pass that way.

When Jesus came to the place and was right under the tree, he looked up and said to him, 'Zacchaeus, hurry and come down; for I must stay at your house today.' So he hurried down and was happy to welcome him. All who saw it began to grumble and said, 'He has gone to be the guest of one who is a sinner.' Zacchaeus stood there and said to the Lord, 'Look, half of my possessions, Lord, I will give to the poor; and if I have lied and tricked anyone to give me money, I will pay back four times as much.'

Then Jesus said to him, 'Today salvation has come to this house, because he too is a son of Abraham. For the Son of Man came to seek out and to save the lost.'

Craft Activity: Rainbow-

This craft makes a rainbow with clouds on one end and a sun on the other. You will need strips of card for each colour of the rainbow. Stick coloured strips together to make a rainbow. Draw a cloud onto white card and a sun onto yellow. Stick sun and clouds at each end of the rainbow. The reason they are making a rainbow is that not everyone is the same. People are different, and like different things. If everyone was the same then life wouldn't be as beautiful. Likewise, if there was only one colour, we wouldn't have rainbows.

Caring: Luke 15:3-7

Jesus told them this story: 'Which one of you, having a hundred sheep and losing one of them, does not leave the ninety-nine in the wilderness where they will stay together for safety and go after the one that is lost until he finds it? When he has found it, he lays it on his shoulders and rejoices. And when he comes home, he calls together his friends and neighbours, saying to them, "Rejoice with me, for I have found my sheep that was lost, and I am so happy to have found it as I care so much about each of my sheep." Just so, I tell you, there will be more joy in heaven over one sinner who repents than over ninety-nine righteous people who need no repentance.

Craft Activity: Sheep Craft-

There are many similar and easily accessible variants of paper sheep crafts. For this you will need to copy the template and cut up a pile of white strips of paper. Cut out sheep front and back. Using the strips of paper fold them into a concertina. Stick between the two halves.

Trust: Proverbs. 3:5 & Exodus 14:19-30

Proverbs 3:5

Trust in the Lord with all your heart,
and do not rely on your own insight.

Exodus 14:19-31

The angel of God who was going before the Israelite army moved and went behind them; and the pillar of cloud moved with it from in front of them and took its place behind them. It came between the army of Egypt and the army of Israel. And so the two armies did not come near the other all night.

God drove the sea back by a strong east wind all night, and turned the sea into dry land; and the waters were divided. The Israelites went into the sea on dry ground, the waters forming a wall for them on their right and on their left. The Egyptians pursued, and went into the sea after them, all of Pharaoh's horses, chariots, and chariot drivers.

At the morning watch the angel of God in the pillar of fire and cloud looked down upon the Egyptian army, and threw the Egyptian army into panic. He clogged their chariot wheels so that they turned with difficulty. The Egyptians said, 'Let us flee from the Israelites, for the Lord is fighting for them against Egypt.'

As the Egyptians fled the Lord tossed the Egyptians into the sea. The waters returned and covered the chariots and the chariot drivers, the entire army of Pharaoh that had followed them into the sea; not one of them remained. But the Israelites walked on dry ground through the sea, the waters forming a wall for them on their right and on their left.

Thus the Lord saved Israel that day from the Egyptians; and Israel saw the Egyptians dead on the seashore. Israel saw the great work that the Lord did against the Egyptians.

Craft Activity: Police hat-

It's always essential that we remind children who they can turn to and trust. Our police should be such people. For this craft they will need the three templates. Print the first two onto dark blue card, the third on normal paper. Cut around the outside, fold on lines and stick brim (template two) so that the black mark lines up with the black mark of template one. Use strips to hold to head. Colour and create symbol for badge. Stick to front of hat.

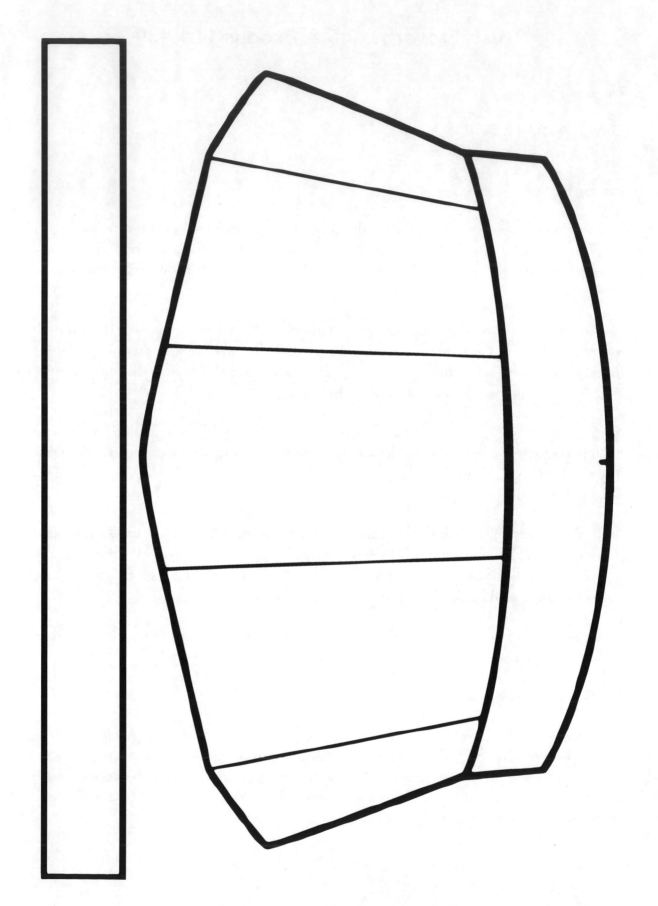

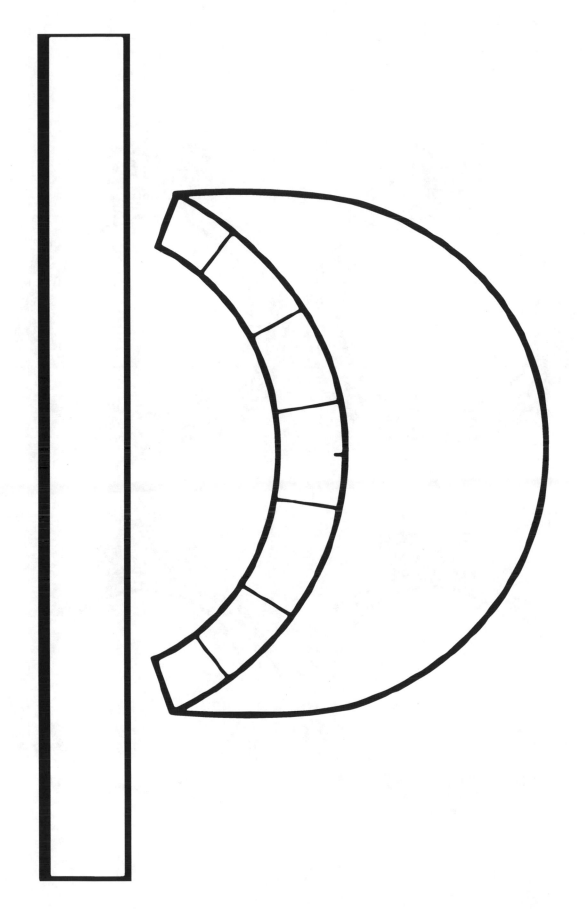

32

Emotion: Ecclesiastes 3:1-8

Everybody has emotions. There are no bad emotions. Emotions are how we feel. This is an opportunity to ask the students what emotions they know. How we act and feel in different situations varies and we all respond differently and feel a little differently. Whilst we affirm that emotions are all normal and natural though, how we respond or act when we are feeling particular emotions may or may not be healthy. It's important then to always find safe and appropriate ways to express how we are feeling.

There is a time and feeling for everything,
and a season for every activity under the heavens in which we will feel all feelings. There is:

a time to be born and a time to die,
a time to plant and a time to uproot,

a time to kill and a time to heal,
a time to tear down and a time to build,

a time to weep and a time to laugh,
a time to mourn and a time to dance,

a time to scatter stones and a time to gather them,
a time to embrace and a time to refrain from embracing,

a time to search and a time to give up,
a time to keep and a time to throw away,

a time to tear and a time to mend,
a time to be silent and a time to speak,

a time to love and a time to hate,
a time for war and a time for peace.

Craft Activity: Fabric Samples glued down to make a little book: when I see this I feel…

The idea of this craft is to show children in a fun and creative way that different feelings can be expressed as colours or tactile surfaces. The children should NOT be told that any colour represents a particular feeling or emotion so that they can express how they find it. All they need to do is cut a bit of fabric and stick it in a square on the template. Each printed page has two pages. Cut each one in half and when they are finished, staple down one side to form a book.

When I see this colour

I feel..........................

When I see this colour

I feel..........................

Royalty: Matthew 22:11

This lesson is a reminder that we should have a healthy sense of self worth and value. As Christians, and heirs with Christ, we are members of his royal household and are invited to acknowledge the innate self-worth in each of us. This lesson uses the story of the wedding banquet to draw attention to the fact that, regardless of background, wealth, status or our previous actions, we are all affirmed and invited to be members of God's family.

The Parable of the Wedding Banquet

Jesus spoke to them again in parables, saying: "The kingdom of heaven is like a king who prepared a wedding reception and feast for his son. He sent his servants to those who had been invited to the wedding reception and feast to tell them to come, but they did not come.

"Then he sent some more servants and said, 'Tell those who have been invited that I have prepared my dinner: My oxen and fattened cattle have been butchered, and everything is ready. Come to the wedding reception and feast.'

"But they paid no attention and went off—one to his field, another to his business. The rest seized his servants, mistreated them and killed them. The king was enraged. He sent his army and destroyed those murderers and burned their city.

"Then he said to his servants, 'the wedding reception and feast is ready, but those I invited did not deserve to come. So go to the street corners and invite to the wedding reception and feast anyone you find.' So the servants went out into the streets and gathered all the people they could find, the bad as well as the good, and the wedding hall was filled with guests.

Craft Activity: Sceptres (a sign of royalty).

Materials:

1. *Styrofoam balls* (about the size of a stress ball/tennis ball)
2. New pencils
3. Paint
4. Glue
5. Feathers
6. Glitter

Get round Styrofoam balls, stab hole in one end of each. Insert pencil into hole. Using a cup to help hold it upright, paint the Styrofoam ball and decorate with glitter. As it is drying, glue on some feathers.

We found that some children finished this quite quickly, while others put more time into patterns and detailing. For those that finished early we provided a paper doll for them to make.

36

Character:

This lesson is a reminder of character and focuses on each child's individual character trying to show each is unique, even if they are similar and are wonderful for being them.

Them

The story this lesson is their story. Going through one child at a time, each child is asked to say one thing that makes the child being described that child. Make sure to do a little on each child and not leave anyone out. Last of all as that child what those their *character* (then say that child's name) like to do more than anything else on the weekend or holidays. Eg. If you had ten children you would start by saying; ' let's talk about 1's character. What can you tell me about 1? What makes 1, 1?' then 2, 3, 4, 5, 6, 7, 8, & 9 all say something about 1.

Craft Activity: Magnifying Glass on Card-

This craft is started by explaining that each person in unique. There will never be another exactly like us. One part that is always just ours even is we have the same colour eyes, or hair or like the same things or wear the same clothes, is our fingerprints.

Materials:

1. *Template*
2. *A variety of coloured card*
3. *Ink*
4. Scissors
5. Pencils or crayons
6. *Glue*

Children will need a copy of the template, colour in the magnifying glass, cut it out and paste it onto another piece of card. They then press their fingertip into the ink and put their fingerprints into the 'glass' area.

Living A Fruitful Life

This is a series of lessons that moves through aspects of a meaningful life that builds purpose, strength of character, and stamina into a child's lived paradigm. Most of the craft ideas are an expression of the lesson topic or model the concept.

Perseverance Hebrews 12:1-11

Key concepts: Elite athletes are very disciplined in their training, enduring strenuous practice routines, because they are focused on the goal of succeeding in their chosen sport. The Bible compares living the Christian life to running a race. Just as running a race wearing a heavy backpack would slow a runner down, so sin gets in the way of our ability to live our lives in a way that honours God. Sin consumes our time and energy and takes our focus off God, slowing us down in our life race. The Bible tells us that God does allow life to get difficult at times so we can be made holy. Even though God's discipline is painful, it produces righteousness and peace. Just as elite athletes push themselves to endure pain during a race by focusing on pre-planned thoughts and goals, we are to rely on Jesus for encouragement and strength when we are running our life race.

God Disciplines His Children

Because we are surrounded by such a great cloud of witnesses: all the ancestors of our people who have come before, let us throw off everything that hinders and the mistakes that lead us to fall short of expectations that so easily entangles. Let us run with perseverance the race marked out for us, fixing our eyes on Jesus, the pioneer and perfecter of faith. For the joy set before him he endured the cross, scorning its shame, and sat down at the right hand of the throne of God. Consider him who endured such opposition from sinners, from people who fell short of what was expected of them, so that you will not grow weary and lose heart.

In your struggle against living up to expectations, you have not yet resisted to the point of shedding your blood because things have been reasonably safe. Have you completely forgotten this word of encouragement that addresses you as a father addresses his son? It says, "My son, do not make light of the Lord's discipline, and do not lose heart when he rebukes you, because the Lord disciplines the one he loves, and he chastens everyone he accepts as his son." Endure hardship as discipline; God is treating you as his children. For what children are not disciplined by their parent or caregiver? If you are not disciplined—and everyone undergoes discipline—then you are not legitimate, not true sons and daughters at all. Moreover, we have all had human parents or caregivers who disciplined us and we respected them for it. How much more should we submit to the Father of spirits and live! Our parents and caregivers disciplined us for a little while as they thought best; but God disciplines us for our good, in order that we may share in his holiness. No discipline seems pleasant at the time, but painful. Later on, however, it produces a harvest of righteousness and peace for those who have been trained by it.

Craft Activity: Origami Rabbit-

Origami is not something that comes naturally and needs to be worked on through the completion of each stage before the finished product is created

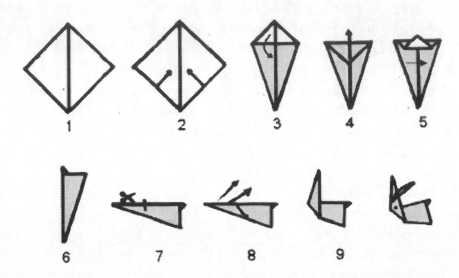

Easy Origami Rabbit Instructions

Take a square sheet of paper and position it so it looks like a diamond shape. Fold in half and unfold.

i.   Fold the bottom left and bottom right edges towards the centre crease. It will look like a kite shape.
ii. Fold the top of the kite (small triangular flap) downwards.
iii. Fold the tip of the kite back up approximately 2/3 of the way. The protruding triangle will be the bunny's tail.
iv. Fold the model in half.
v.   Rotate clockwise a quarter turn.
vi. Cut the top crease a little less than half the length of the paper.
vii. Fold the two flaps upwards to make ears.
viii. Curl the ears and decorate with eyes.

Don't Be Lazy Proverbs 6:6-8 / Proverbs 26:13-17.

sluggard

noun: **sluggard***; plural noun:* **sluggards**

a lazy, sluggish person.

Key Concept: We can learn from the ants and become wise. The ants do their work even when they don't have someone telling them what to do or checking up on them.

Go to the ant and watch it, you sluggard; consider its ways and be wise! It has no commander, no overseer or ruler, yet it works hard, stores its provisions in summer and gathers its food at harvest. A sluggard says, "There's a lion in the road, a fierce lion roaming the streets!" As a door turns on its hinges, so a sluggard turns on his bed. A sluggard buries their hand in the food bowl; but is then too lazy to bring it back to their mouth to eat the food. A sluggard is wiser in their own eyes than seven people who answer discreetly. Like one who grabs a stray dog by the ears a sluggard is someone who rushes into a quarrel not their own. They do not think carefully first or show the initiative in trying to get things done.

Craft Activity: Ants.

Materials:

1. *Black cirlces (three per child)*
2. *Card*
3. *Glue*
4. Eyes (two pcr child)
5. Pencils or crayons

Children will need to glue their three black circles in a line onto the card with each circle just touching the one before it. Six legs need to be drawn: three on each side, and two antenna on the head. Stick the two eyes to the head. They should end up looking like the one in the picture below.

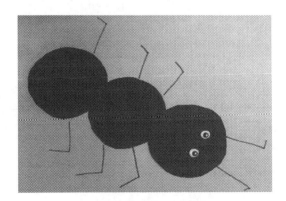

Right Priorities Mark 10:17-31

Key Concept: Children will discover that special priority should be given to Jesus every day of our life. What counts can't always be counted; what can be counted doesn't always count. Applying this to work today requires real sensitivity and honesty with regard to our own instincts and values. Wealth is sometimes a result of work — ours or someone else's — but work itself can also be an emotional obstacle to following Jesus. If we have privileged positions — as the rich man did —managing our careers may become more important than serving others, doing good work, or even making time for family, civic and spiritual life. It may hinder us from opening ourselves to an unexpected calling from God. Our wealth and privilege may make us arrogant or insensitive to the people around us.

The Rich Man

As Jesus was setting out on a journey, a man ran up and knelt before him, and asked him, 'Good Teacher, what must I do to inherit eternal life?' Jesus said to him, 'Why do you call me good? No one is good but God alone. You know the commandments: "You shall not murder; You shall not commit adultery; You shall not steal; You shall not bear false witness; You shall not defraud; Honour your father and mother."' He said to him, 'Teacher, I have kept all these since I was a young man.' Jesus, looking at him, loved him and said; 'You lack one thing; right priorities. So go, sell what you own, and give the money to the poor, and you will have treasure and rewards in heaven; then come and follow me.' When he heard this, the man was shocked and went away grieving, for he had many possessions.

Then Jesus looked around and said to his disciples, 'How hard it will be for those who have wealth to enter the kingdom of God!' And the disciples were perplexed at these words. But Jesus said to them again, 'Children, how hard it is to enter the kingdom of God! It is easier for a camel to go through the eye of a needle than for someone who is rich to enter the kingdom of God.' They were greatly astounded and said to one another, 'Then who can be saved?' Jesus looked at them and said, 'For mortals it is impossible, but not for God; for God all things are possible.'

Peter began to say to him, 'Look, we have left everything and followed you.' Jesus said, 'Truly I tell you, there is no one who has left house or brothers or sisters or mother or father or children or fields, for my sake and for the sake of the Kingdom, who will not receive a hundredfold now in this age—houses, brothers and sisters, mothers and children, and fields, with persecutions—and in the age to come eternal life. But many who are first will be last, and the last will be first.'

Craft Activity: House Craft-

Children will need a copy of the house template. They need to colour it in and cut it out. Fold on lines and glue tabs.

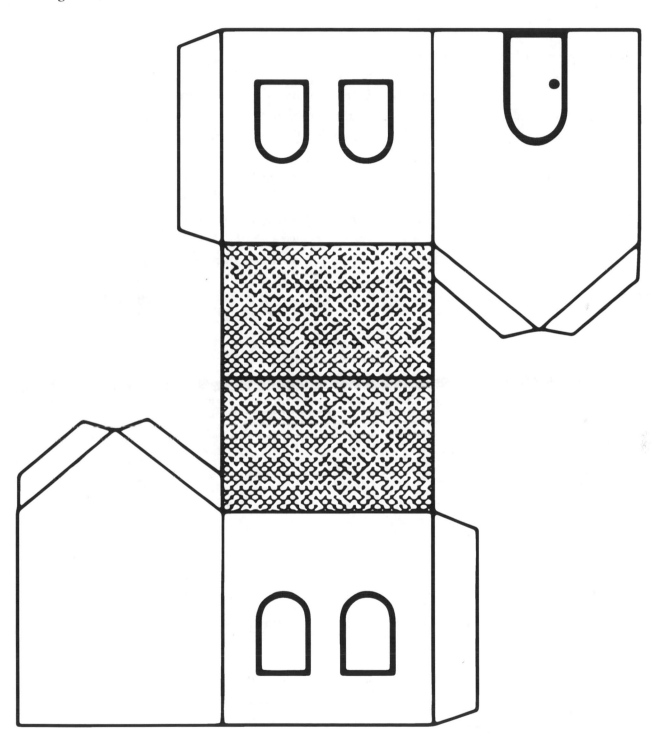

Don't Waste Your Talent 1 Corinthians 12:4-31

Key Concept: All Spiritual Gifts are given to us from God, for the building up of the Church.

One Body with Many Members

Now there are varieties of gifts, of talents that people have, but it is the same Spirit; and there are varieties of services people can do, but the same Lord they do them for; and there are varieties of activities people can participate in, but it is the same God who activates all of them in everyone.

To each is given the manifestation of the Spirit for the common good. To one is given through the Spirit the utterance of wisdom, and to another the utterance of knowledge according to the same Spirit, to another faith by the same Spirit, to another gifts of healing by the one Spirit, to another the working of miracles, to another prophecy, to another the discernment of spirits, to another various kinds of tongues, to another the interpretation of tongues.

All these and many more gifts and talents are activated by one and the same Spirit, who allots to each one individually just as the Spirit chooses.

Our community is made up of many differently talented people so there should be no dissension within the body, but all members should have the same care for one another. If one member suffers, all suffer together with it; if one member is honoured, all rejoice together with it.

Craft Activity: Holy Spirit Dove Plate-

Materials:

1. *Paper plate*
2. *Paint: red, yellow, orange*
3. *Glue*
4. Scissors
5. Glitter
6. Clingwrap (cut up to be slightly larger than plate and one for each child)
7. Dove template

Children will need to be careful of getting paint on their clothes. Give each child a plate. Squirt one blob of red, yellow and orange onto their plates. Give them cling wrap. Get them to lay cling wrap over plate and squish and smear the paint around. Sprinkle with glitter. Cut out dove and have them place the dove onto the centre of the plate.

Heavenly Treasures Matthew 13:44-49

Key Concept: Children will learn that there is a wonderful place called Heaven, which is a greater treasure than anything else in the world.

Three Parables

'The kingdom of heaven is like treasure hidden in a field, which someone found when no one was looking and then re-hid; then in excitement and joy they go and sells all that they have and then buys that field.

'Again, the kingdom of heaven is like a merchant in search of fine pearls;
on finding one pearl of great value, the merchant went and sold all that they had and used the money to buy the pearl.

'Again, the kingdom of heaven is like a net that fishermen threw into the sea and caught fish of every kind; when it was full, they drew it ashore, sat down, and put the good into baskets but threw out the bad. So it will be at the end of the age. The angels will come out and separate the evil from the righteous.

Craft Activity: Treasure Chest-

Children will need a copy of the template. Have children colour and decorate their chest, cut out, fold and glue down tabs.

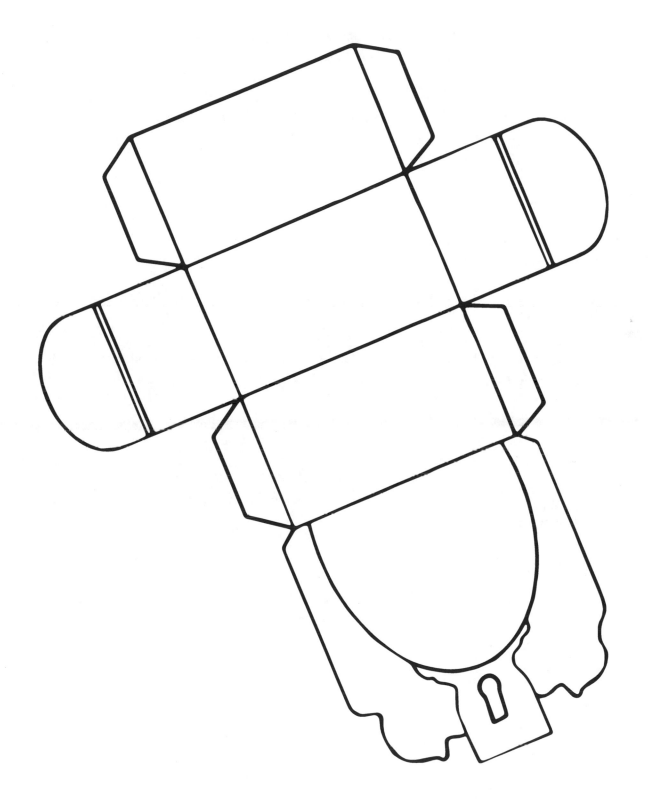

Count Your Blessings Job 37:14-19

*The **cornucopia** (from Latin cornu copiae) or horn of plenty is a symbol of abundance, prosperity and nourishment, and is commonly depicted as a large horn-shaped container overflowing with produce, flowers or nuts. Key Concepts: Everything received from God that brings joy and happiness is a blessing. The aim of this lesson is to try and draw the children's minds to the things that they have and should be thankful for but take for granted. Children may even be encouraged to say 'thankyou' to their parents or caregivers for looking after and providing for them.*

Listen and Consider

'Job, listen and hear this;
stop what you are doing and consider the wondrous works of God.

Do you know how God lays his command upon the clouds and causes the lightning of his cloud to shine?

Or do you know the balancings of the clouds, the wondrous works of God, the one whose knowledge is perfect, you whose garments are hot when the earth is still because of the south wind?

Can you Job, like God, spread out the skies, vast and unyielding as a cast mirror?

Teach us what we shall say to him; we cannot draw up our case because of darkness. We do not know the things beyond our comprehension, but we can know of the wonderful abundance to which we are a part.

Craft Activity: Horn of plenty-

Children will need to colour their horn in cut it out. Rolling it into a cone, cover the blank space with the pattern. Have the childrenthen fill it with potpourri of lavender.

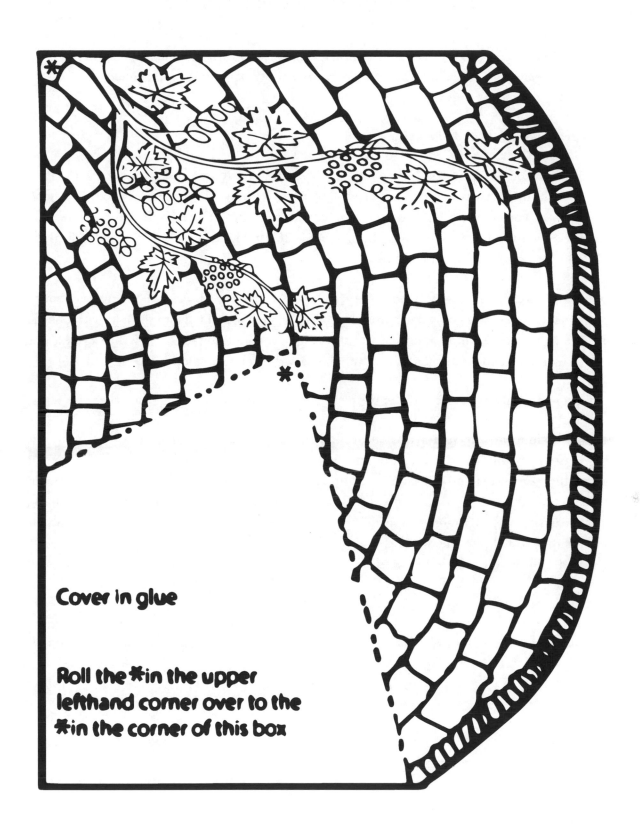

Cover in glue

Roll the *in the upper
lefthand corner over to the
*in the corner of this box

Be a Good Example Luke 10:25-37

This lesson is designed to focus on copying/emulating positive behaviour and appropriate role models. It is also an opportunity to remind people to to jump to conclusions and judge without knowing someone.

The Parable of the Good Samaritan

Once a lawyer stood up to test Jesus. 'Teacher,' he said, 'what must I do to inherit eternal life?' He said to him, 'What is written in the law? What do you read there?' He answered, 'You shall love the Lord your God with all your heart, and with all your soul, and with all your strength, and with all your mind; and your neighbour as yourself.' And he said to him, 'You have given the right answer; do this, and you will live.'

But wanting to explain himself and get a deeper answer, he asked Jesus, 'And who is my neighbour?' Jesus replied, 'A man was going down from Jerusalem to Jericho, and fell into the hands of robbers, who stripped him, beat him, and went away, leaving him half dead. Now by chance a priest was going down that road; and when he saw him, he passed by on the other side.

So likewise a Levite, when he came to the place and saw him, passed by on the other side.

But a Samaritan while travelling came near him; and when he saw him, he was moved with pity. He went to him and bandaged his wounds, having poured oil and wine on them. Then he put him on his own animal, brought him to an inn, and took care of him. The next day he took out two denarii,[b] gave them to the innkeeper, and said, "Take care of him; and when I come back, I will repay you whatever more you spend." Which of these three, do you think, was a neighbour to the man who fell into the hands of the robbers?' He said, 'The one who showed him mercy.' Jesus said to him, 'Go and do likewise.'

Craft Activity: Medical Bag-

Print out templates and have children colour in their medical bag and place their equipment inside.

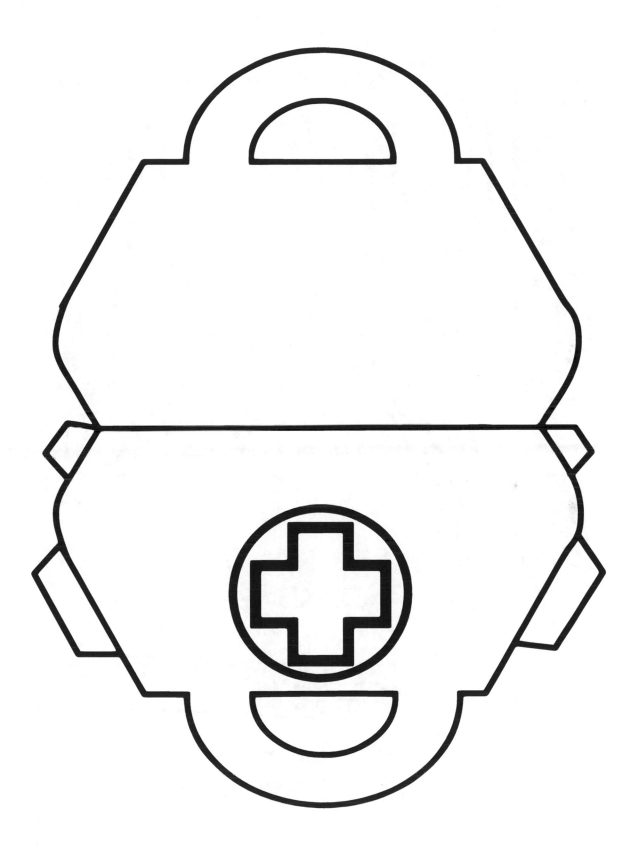

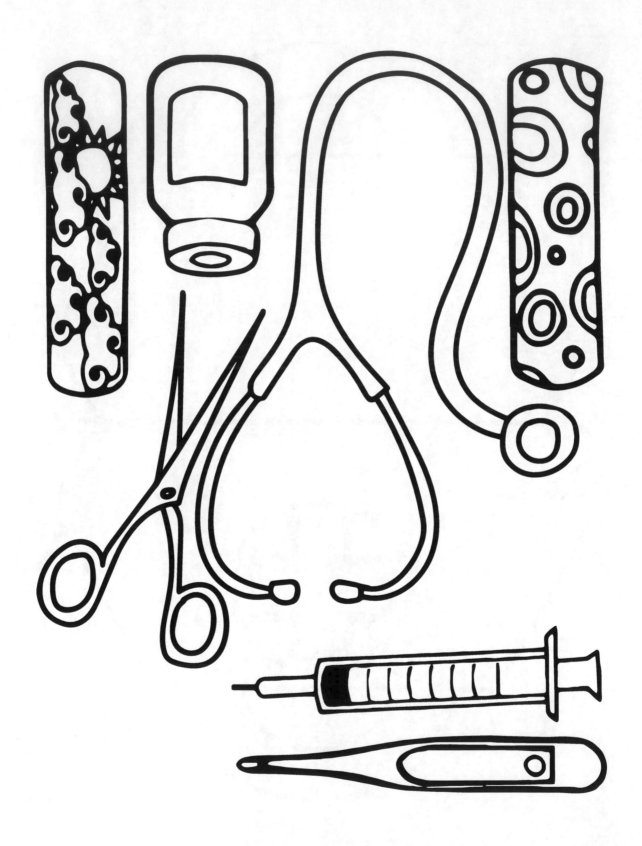

Walk the Narrow Path Matthew 7:13

Following on from the lesson on being a good example, this lesson is designed to have children think about how easy it is to follow the crowd, to copy and behave like all the popular people are. Draw out in conversation with them what it means to do the right thing and stand up for what they believe, perhaps (if you feel confident) talk about bullying and the effects of peer pressure, had how important it is to stand firm in their beliefs.

The Narrow Gate

'In everything, regardless of what you are doing, do to others as you would have them do to you; treat others as you would like them to be treating you; for this is what all the laws are about and what all the prophets and wise men have tried to teach. Remember, 'Enter through the narrow gate; for the gate is wide and the road is easy that leads to bad things and destruction, and there are many who take it. For the gate is narrow and the road is hard that leads to life and doing the right thing, and there are few who find it.

Craft Activity: Building an archway. You will need to print the template onto card and the children may need help in carefully sticking the different sections together. Fold along dotted lines and apply glue to the tabs.

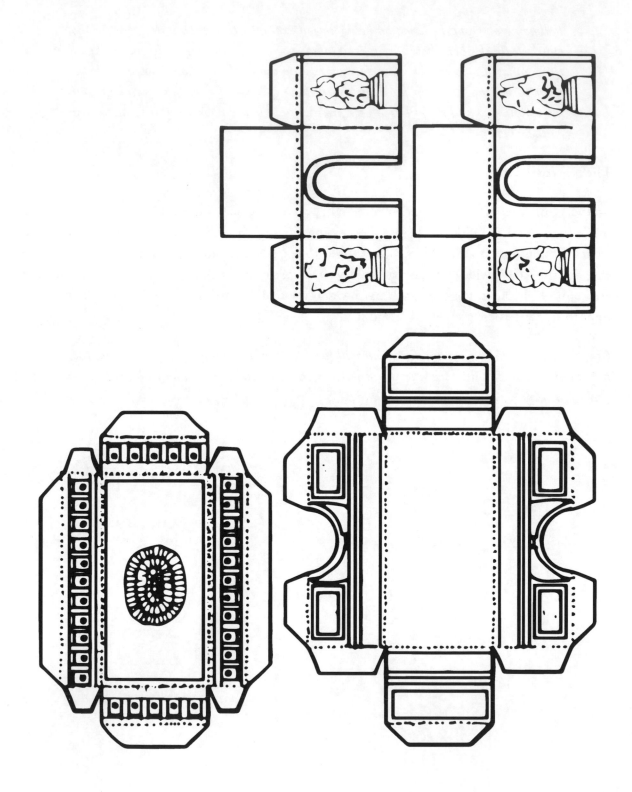

Success

This is a series of lessons that looks at, and encourages growth in, successful living and what a successful life should be like, regardless of what we have, or get.

Self Control Genesis 26:17-22

Isaac moved away and encamped in the Valley of Gerar, where he settled. Isaac reopened the wells that had been dug in the time of his father Abraham, which the Philistines had stopped up after Abraham died, and he gave them the same names his father had given them.

Isaac's servants dug in the valley and discovered a well of fresh water there. But the herders of Gerar quarreled with those of Isaac and said, "The water is ours!" So he named the well Esek, (which means *dispute)* because they disputed with him.

Then they dug another well, but they quarreled over that one also; so he named it Sitnah.*(which means opposition).*

He moved on from there and dug another well, and no one quarreled over it. He named it Rehoboth,*(which means room).* saying, "Now the Lord has given us room and we will flourish in the land."

Craft Activity: Paper Cup Dragon.

This dragon cup craft is based off a breathing exercise used in counselling sessions with children. When the child blows through the hole in the bottom of the cup, the streamers taped to the front of the cup blow around to create a fire-breathing dragon whilst at the same time causing the child to take deep breaths and breathe slowly

We talked about how sometimes our heart starts pounding and we feel like we cannot control ourselves. One way to help us chill out is by dragon breathing. To take a dragon breath, we breathe in deep through our nose, hold it for a few seconds, then release a hot fiery breath from our mouths.

Materials:

1. *Paper cup*
2. *Coloured paper*
3. *Glue and tape*
4. Scissors
5. Red and yellow streamers
6. textas

Poke a hole in the bottom of the cup with the scissors. Cut the streamers to approx. 20cm in length and stick to inside of cup. Cut coloured paper to fit around outside of cup and glue on. Use the textas to draw eyes, or make some out of paper and stick up near the 'mouth'. Tuck the streamers into the 'mouth'. When children blow into the hole at the back of the cup, the 'fire' should come alive.

Stillness 1 Kings 19: 1-13

King Ahab and Jezebel his queen were evil people and killed nearly all the good prophets, except Elijah. Jezebel sent a messenger to Elijah saying; "May the gods deal with me, be it ever so severely, if by this time tomorrow I do not make your life like that of one of them."

Elijah was afraid and ran for his life. When he came to Beersheba in Judah he went a day's journey into the wilderness. He came to a broom bush, sat down under it and prayed that he might die. "I have had enough, Lord," he said. "Take my life; I am no better than my ancestors." Then he lay down under the bush and fell asleep.

All at once an angel touched him and said, "Get up and eat." He looked around, and there by his head was some bread baked over hot coals, and a jar of water. He ate and drank and then lay down again. The angel came back a second time and touched him and said, "Get up and eat, for the journey is too much for you." So he got up and ate and drank. Strengthened by that food, he travelled forty days and forty nights until he reached Horeb, the mountain of God. There he went into a cave and spent the night.

God said; "What are you doing here, Elijah?"

He replied, "I have been very zealous for you but the Israelites have rejected your covenant, torn down your altars, and put your prophets to death with the sword. I am the only one left, and now they are trying to kill me too."

God said; "Go out and stand on the mountain in my presence for I am about to pass by." Then a great and powerful wind tore the mountains apart and shattered the rocks before the Lord, but the God was not in the wind. After the wind there was an earthquake, but God was not in the earthquake. After the earthquake came a fire, but God was not in the fire. And after the fire came a gentle whisper. When Elijah heard it, he pulled his cloak over his face and went out and stood at the mouth of the cave.

Craft: Stop/Slow Signs-

This lesson is designed to remind children that life can get really busy and hectic and that there is so much we miss and will miss if we don't stop and slow down. It's a time to explain to children that all the realty important things are in the small moments of our lives. Print out the two templates and colour. Cut and paste back to back sticking the Stop and Slow onto opposite sides.

Slow

Stop

Learning Patience Genesis 17:1-6, 17

Abraham & Sarah

When Abram was ninety-nine years old the Lord God appeared to Abram and said to him; 'I am God almighty; walk before me and be blameless, that I may make my covenant between me and you, and may multiply you greatly.' Then Abram fell on his face. And God said to him, 'Behold, my covenant is with you, and you shall be the father of a multitude of nations. No longer shall your name be called Abram, but your name shall me Abraham, for I have made you the father of a multitude of nations. I will make you exceedingly fruitful, and I will make you into nations, and kings shall come from you.' Then Abraham fell on his face and laughed and said to himself; 'After all this time, shall a child be born to a man who is a hundred years old? Shall Sarah, who is ninety years old, bear even one child?'"

Sometimes God asks us to wait for something even though he's promised it to us. God promised Abraham he would be the father of many people. But at a very old age, he was still without any children. Abraham and Sarah knew what God had told them but they had yet to see evidence of the promise in their lives. How could Abraham become the father of many when he didn't have any children? Abraham and Sarah trusted God and they waited patiently for him. This doesn't mean they waited perfectly. They took matters into their own hands at times. But God's grace covered them and he still fulfilled his promise, in his perfect timing.

Sometimes God and parents ask us to wait for things. We have to trust that they know what is best for us and will do what they promised. As we wait, it can be tempting to make things happen on our own or to run ahead. But waiting patiently means waiting without question or complaining.

Craft: Bingo Game.

Children cut out and stick numbers to their board. Explain that everyone will finish and get a prize but they must wait until all their numbers have been called out.

1	2	3	4	5	6	7	8	9	10
11	12	13	14	15	16	17	18	19	20
21	22	23	24	25	26	27	28	29	30
31	32	33	34	35	36	37	38	39	40
41	42	43	44	45	46	47	48	49	50
51	52	53	54	55	56	57	58	59	60
61	62	63	64	65	66	67	68	69	70
71	72	73	74	75	76	77	78	79	80
81	82	83	84	85	86	87	88	89	90
91	92	93	94	95	96	97	98	99	100

Willpower Matthew 4:1-11

How many times have you heard someone say; "I wish I had more will-power or self-control!" Maybe you have said it or wished it yourself? Most people feel they don't have enough self-control. The Bible is speaks on its importance; "Like a city whose walls are broken through is a person who lacks self-control" (Proverbs 25:28).

So what is self-control? The phrase seems to imply a hefty dose of sheer willpower. And there is, indeed, work involved.

Peter writes, "Make every effort to add to your faith goodness; and to goodness, knowledge; and to knowledge, self-control; and to self-control, perseverance; and to perseverance, godliness; and to godliness, mutual affection; and to mutual affection, love" (2 Peter 1:5-7).

To learn takes attentiveness—and humility. We have to trust that our teacher knows more than we do. We need to accept that perhaps the lessons aren't going to be entertaining, relaxing or humorous. They may not satisfy our obvious desires, but, rather, lead our hearts toward deeper ones.

Jesus Is Tested in the Wilderness

Then Jesus was quickly led by the Spirit into the wilderness to be tempted by the devil. After not eating for forty days and forty nights, he was hungry. The devil came to him and said, "If you are the Son of God, tell these stones to become bread."

Jesus answered, "It is written: 'Man shall not live on bread alone, but on every word that comes from the mouth of God.'"

Then the devil took him to the holy city and had him stand on the highest point of the temple. "If you are the Son of God," he said, "throw yourself down. For it is written:

"'He will command his angels concerning you,

and they will lift you up in their hands,

so that you will not strike your foot against a stone.'"

Jesus answered him, "It is also written: 'Do not put the Lord your God to the test.'"

After that, the devil took him to a very high mountain and showed him all the kingdoms of the world and their splendour. "All this I will give you," he said, "if you will bow down and worship me."

Jesus said to him, "Away from me, Satan! For it is written: 'Worship the Lord your God, and serve him only.'"

Then the devil left him, and angels came and attended him.

Craft: Koi Fish-

Koi carp are symbolic of willpower, perseverance and strength of purpose. Colour the koi fish in, cut out and paste the two sides together. Stick bright streamers to the bottom end.

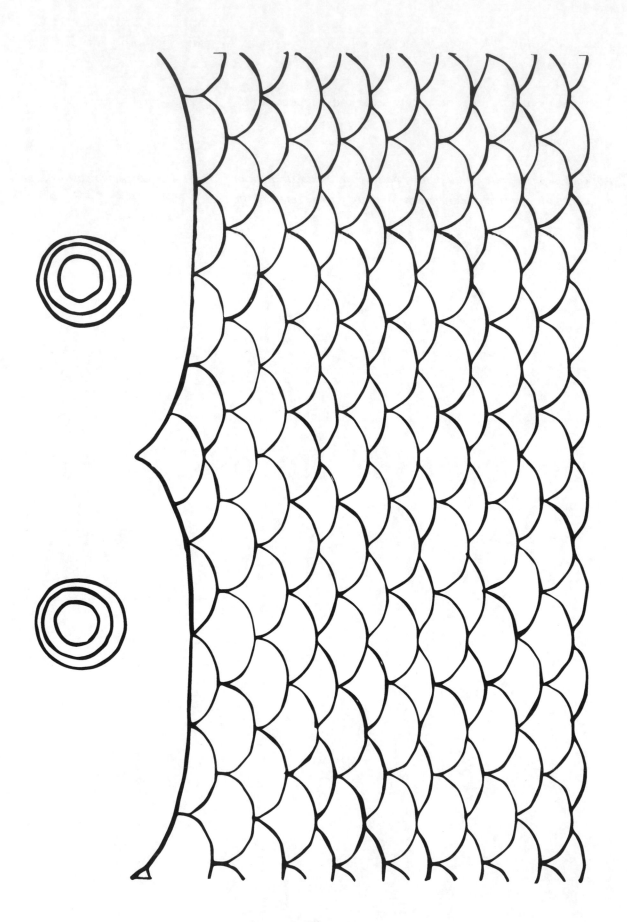

Bravery Ezra, chapters 7-8

Once upon a time, a man named Ezra had to go on a lengthy journey through places where robbers and bandits lurked. Just how did Ezra get himself into such a scary situation? It all started a long, long time ago.

Ezra lived at a time when the people of Israel had been taken captive and were living in a foreign land. In this other country, they were forced to serve the king of the land. After the Israelites had lived for many years in this foreign land, God decided to allow the Israelites to return to Jerusalem, their special city where they had lived before being taken captive. The Israelites wanted to rebuild the temple in Jerusalem so they could worship God there again. A man named Artaxerxes was king at that time and the Bible says that "The king had granted Ezra everything he asked, for the hand of his God was on him." King Artaxerxes gave permission for Ezra and anyone else to return to Jerusalem. He also sent gold and silver along with Ezra and instructed him to buy rams and bulls to offer to His God as a sacrifice in Jerusalem. Artaxerxes also sent a letter with Ezra telling the governors of the areas where Ezra was going to give Ezra more money, wheat and oil and salt if he needed it. The king also told Ezra that it was his job to teach all of the other Israelites to follow God's laws as he did. Ezra knew this was a big job and that the journey to Jerusalem would be dangerous. Ezra and the men going with him were also taking their wives and children and all that they owned. They did not travel in cars, but in wagons and on foot. The journey would take a long, long time and along the roads there could be thieves waiting to steal their possessions or enemies waiting to hurt them.

Even though the journey would be scary, Ezra praised God anyway and thanked Him for the honour of serving Him. Ezra said; "Because the hand of the Lord my God was on me, I took courage and gathered leading men from Israel to go up with me" (Ezra 7:28).

Ezra was tempted to ask the king for soldiers to protect them on their journey, but he was ashamed to do so, because he had told the king that God would take care of them (Ezra 8:22). Instead of asking for soldiers, they fasted and prayed and asked God to protect them on their journey. And God did! Ezra and his men and their families arrived safely in Jerusalem. Ezra was glad and sang joyfully;, "The hand of our God was on us, and He protected us from enemies and bandits along the way."

Badger

The badger is known for being an animal that won't back down in the face of danger. Its muscular neck and thick, loose fur protect it when an animal predator strikes. These defence mechanisms give it time to turn on the predator and bite or claw it. When a badger is attacked, it also uses vocalizations. It hisses, growls, squeals and snarls. It also releases an unpleasant smell that may drive a predator away.

Badgers are particularly courageous when they are threatened, facing their enemies with fearlessness. They simply won't back down, even when threatened by a much larger animal! Despite their reputation for being fierce, these animals would not go out of their way to harm a person. Like most wild animals, they choose to avoid people. People are a much larger threat to these animals than these creatures are to humans.

Craft: Badger mask

Success/Achieving Goals

When we set goals in life we need to actually achieve them. There is no point in saying; 'I'll do this', or " I'll do that' and never actually doing it. In Genesis we read that the favour of God was on Joseph's life and that God gave him dreams and a vision to do great things.

The Story of Joseph

Joseph was seventeen and had eleven brothers: ten older and one younger than him.

Because Joseph was one of the youngest sons, his father spent more time with him, and he became very special to him. So his father, Jacob, had a special robe made for Joseph. All of Joseph's older brothers saw this and they got very jealous. They got so jealous they couldn't even say a kind word to him, which was not very nice.

One day Joseph had a dream, and he told his brothers; "Guess what? Last night I had a strange dream. We were tying up bunches of grain out in the field when suddenly my bunch stood up, while all of yours gathered around and bowed to me." The brothers looked at each other in disgust, but Joseph continued. "Then I had another dream that the sun, moon, and eleven stars bowed down to me."

"Who do you think you are?" The brothers said. "Do you think that you are better than all of us? Do you think that we would ever bow down to you?" This made the brothers dislike Joseph even more. When he told his father about his dreams he said, "Those are strange dreams." But he thought carefully about what Joseph had told him.

A few days later Joseph's father asked him to check on his brothers. They were in the fields quite a distance away. So Joseph went to find them.

When the brothers saw Joseph in the distance, they made a plan to kill him. But when Reuben, Joseph's oldest brother heard this he said, "Let's not kill him, just throw him in a well out here in the field." He said this because he was secretly planning to come back and rescue Joseph when the other brothers had left.

So when Joseph came to them, they took off his beautiful robe and they threw him in an empty well. A little while later a group of people came by that were wanting to sell some things in Egypt. One of the brothers spoke up, "Why don't we sell him to these people, this way we never have to see him again, and we don't have to kill him." So they sold Joseph to the people going to Egypt. They took Joseph's beautiful robe and dipped it in animal blood and took it back to their father. When the father saw this he cried, "Some animal has killed my son." And he cried for many days, so much that nobody could comfort him.

Now Joseph had started out as a slave, but the Lord was with Joseph and He helped him do everything right. Potiphar, the Egyptian who had bought Joseph made him his helper, and put him in charge of everything that he owned. But when Potiphar's wife lied about Joseph Potiphar had Joseph put into jail.

After Joseph had been in jail for some time a cupbearer and baker to Pharaoh had been sent there. One night each of them had a dream. They told their dreams to Joseph and he told the cupbearer that he would soon be let out of jail. "Please tell Pharaoh about me, and ask him to get me out of here." Joseph said.

When the cupbearer was freed he forgot about what Joseph did. So Joseph stayed in jail for two more years. Until one day the Pharaoh had a dream, and nobody could explain it to him. The cupbearer then remembered what Joseph had done for him, and Joseph was brought to Pharaoh.

"Can you understand dreams?" Pharaoh asked. "With Gods' help." Joseph replied. Pharaoh told Joseph his dream. Joseph explained, "God is warning you. There will be seven years when nothing will grow and there will be no food."

"What can I do?" Pharaoh asked. "God has shown you. There will be seven years before the bad years that will be very good and there will be extra food. Save a little each year, that way you will have enough to get you through the bad years." Joseph said.

Pharaoh believed all that Joseph told him, and put him in charge of all the land of Egypt.

When the seven bad years arrived, people came from all countries to buy grain from Joseph. Some of those people were Joseph's brothers. Because it had been over 10 years since they had seen him they didn't recognise him. Joseph recognized them!

The brothers all bowed to him because he was an important person. Just as he dreamed they would. After a few meetings with his brothers he could not keep it in any longer and Joseph said to his brothers, "I am Joseph! Is my father alive?" But his brothers couldn't answer him because they were afraid. Then Joseph said, "Come here. I am your brother, the one you sold! Do not worry, and do not be angry at yourselves for selling me, because God has put me here to save people from starving."

So his father, his brothers, and their families came to live in Egypt with Joseph, and they had all the food they needed.

You may not be exactly sure what the plan is for your life. The important thing to realize is that you do have a purpose, need to set goals for what you want to do, and make that happen. If you trust in God to help you and work hard for your dreams, you can be sure that no matter what business you're in, you'll be headed in the right direction. Do you think Joseph wanted to end up as a slave sold by his brothers? I don't think so. But Joseph trusted God and worked hard in his current situation, which led him to greater work and responsibilities.

Craft: A Twine Star-

The children make a star as we reach for the stars as a metaphor for reaching out to catch our dreams, goals and ambitions.

Materials:

1. *Star template*
2. *pen*
3. *Craft Glue*
4. Scissors
5. Twine/string (2 ply)
6. cardboard

Print and cut out the star template on to cardboard. Glue the end of the twine down at one of the "v"'s of the star. Start winding your twine tightly around the star, gluing as you go around the body of the star Don't worry about the tips of your star right now. Continue all the way around your star with the twine, gluing as you go, until you get to the place where you started. Cut your twine and glue the end down or tuck it under the twine.

For the tips glue the end of twine over the tip of the star and let dry for a minute or two. This will hide the end. Start wrapping your twine around the tip, gluing as you go, until you get as far down as you want to go. Tuck under the end and glue. Repeat for the remaining tips. Glue on a hanging loop.

Humility Luke18:10-14

The Parable of the Tax Collector and the Pharisee

"Two men went up to the Temple to pray, one was a Pharisee who was an important person who always did the right thing, and the other was a tax collector who would take extra money when he should not have from people.

The Pharisee stood up and prayed about himself: 'God, I thank you that I am not like other men-robbers, evildoers, adulterers-or even like this tax collector. I fast twice a week and give a tenth of all I get.'

"But the tax collector stood at a distance. He would not even look up to heaven, but beat his breast and said, 'God, have mercy on me, a sinner, I have doe=ne the wrong thing and I am sorry.' "I tell you that this man, rather than the other, went home justified before God. For everyone who exalts himself will be humbled, and he who humbles himself will be exalted."

"One of the advantages of humility is that it enables us to learn from everyone. A proud person cannot learn from other people because he feels he already knows better than they. On the other hand, a humble person who respects everyone has the openness of mind to learn from everyone and every situation. Just as water cannot collect on mountain peaks, so good qualities and blessings cannot gather on the rocky peaks of pride. If, instead, we maintain a humble, respectful attitude toward everyone, good qualities and inspiration will flow into our mind all the time, like streams flowing into a valley."

Materials:

1. *White paper*
2. *Paper plate (or other means to trace a circle)*
3. *Sticky tape*
4. Scissors
5. Colouring pencils or crayons

Help children to trace and cut out a circle. After that, cut out a triangle equal to around one quarter of the circle. With that "pac man" shape, draw a rocky mountain on one side and a valley meadow with lots of growth on the other. The alignment might be tricky for young ones but the pictures or an example will help. After that, simply connect up the edge and sticky tape to form the cone.

Forgiveness Luke 15:11-32

1: the act of excusing a mistake or offense

2: compassionate feelings that support a willingness to forgive

Jesus loved to tell people about God's forgiveness. One story Jesus told was the saddest. It spoke of a boy who left his father's home, taking all his money and everything he had. In a country far away the boy spent his money foolishly until it was all gone. Now what could he do? To make matters worse, a famine came so there was no food. The boy could starve to death.

Desperate with hunger, the boy got a job feeding pigs. But no one fed him. He would have eaten the pig's food gladly, and perhaps he did when no one was looking.

Finally, the boy came to his senses. "Back home, even the servants eat well," he thought.

"I'll go home and tell Father I'm sorry for my sins. I'm not worthy to be his son anymore. I hope he'll hire me as a servant."

While the boy was still a long way from home, his father saw him coming. Joyously, the father ran to his returning son. He kissed the boy, and hugged him.

"Father, I have sinned. I'm not worthy to be your son." The boy wanted to ask his father to hire him as a servant. But the Father interrupted. "Bring the best robe, sandals, and a ring for my son. And prepare for a great party."

There was a wonderful party because the son who was lost had been found.

Craft activity: Pig Worksheet-

Colour the pig in. Cut out each bit. Roll rectangle to make a cylinder and stick. Stand the cylinder upright. This is the body. Glue the face, feet and tail to body.

Sharing John 6:1–13

Jesus Feeds the Five Thousand

Once, Jesus crossed to the far shore of the Sea of Galilee (that is, the Sea of Tiberias), and a great crowd of people followed him because they saw the signs he had performed by healing the sick. Then Jesus went up on a mountainside and sat down with his disciples. The Jewish Passover Festival was near.

When Jesus looked up and saw a great crowd coming toward him, he said to Philip, "Where shall we buy bread for these people to eat?" He asked this only to test him, for he already had in mind what he was going to do, but also because he realised that nobody had thought to bring enough to eat with them.

Philip answered him, "It would take more than half a year's wages to buy enough bread for each one to have a bite!"

Another of his disciples, Andrew, Simon Peter's brother, spoke up, "Here is a boy with five small barley loaves and two small fish, but how far will they go among so many?"

Jesus said, "Have the people sit down." There was plenty of grass in that place, and they sat down (about five thousand men were there). Jesus then took the loaves, gave thanks, and distributed to those who were seated as much as they wanted. He did the same with the fish.

When they had all had enough to eat, he said to his disciples, "Gather the pieces that are left over. Let nothing be wasted." So they gathered them and filled twelve baskets with the pieces of the five barley loaves left over by those who had eaten.

Craft activity: Loaves and Fish in Basket-

Colour and cut out the bread, fish and two sides of the basket. Staple the basket together so that the fish and bread can sit in the top.

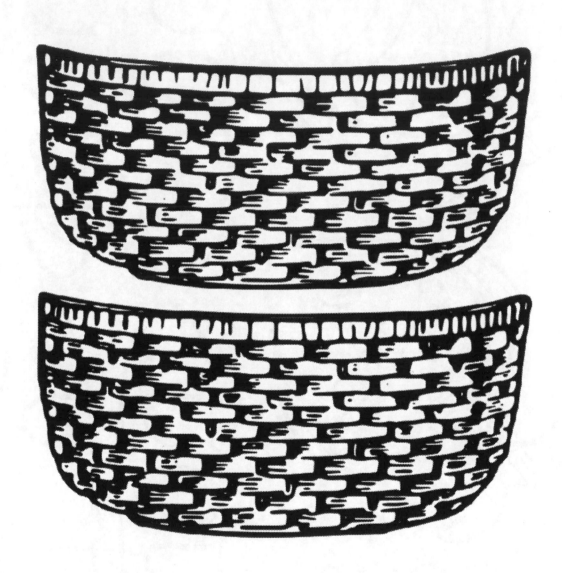

Communal Living

This is a series of lessons that attempts to engage people in how they should be with others: both in their familial lives and communal lives.

Helping and healing John 5:1-15

A Man Healed at the Pool of Bethesda

There was a feast of the Jews, and Jesus went up to Jerusalem for this party. Now there is in Jerusalem by the Sheep Gate a pool, which is called in Hebrew, Bethesda, and it has five porches.

In these lay a great multitude of sick people, blind, lame, paralysed, waiting for the moving of the water. For an angel went down at a certain time into the pool and stirred up the water; and then whoever stepped in first, after the stirring of the water, was made well of whatever disease they had. Now a certain man was there who had an infirmity thirty-eight years. When Jesus saw him lying there, and knew that he already had been in that condition a long time, He said to him, "Do you want to be made well?"

The sick man answered Him, "Sir, I have no one to put me into the pool when the water is stirred up; but while I am coming, another steps down before me."

Jesus said to him, "Rise, take up your bed and walk." And immediately the man was made well, took up his bed, and walked.

And that day was the Sabbath, the day people were supposed to be resting. The Jews therefore said to the man who was cured, "It is the Sabbath; it is not lawful for you to carry your bed."

He answered them, "There was a man who just made me well said to me, 'Take up your bed and walk.'"

Then they asked him, "Who is the man who said to you, 'Take up your bed and walk'?" But the one who was healed did not know who it was, for Jesus had withdrawn and disappeared into the crowed, for lots of people were in that place. Afterward Jesus found him in the temple, and spoke to him.

The man departed and told the Jews that it was Jesus who had made him well.

Craft: Heart Template-

Print out the heart template and insert people/animals we care about/who care about us.

Inclusion 1 Corinthians 12:12-27

One Body with Many Members

For just as the body is one and has many members, and all the members of the body, though many, are one body, so it is with Christ. For in one Spirit we were all baptized into one body—Jews or Greeks, slaves or free—and all were made to drink of one Spirit.

For the body does not consist of one member but of many. If the foot should say, "Because I am not a hand, I do not belong to the body," that would not make it any less a part of the body at all for it is still connected. And if the ear should say, "Because I am not an eye, I do not belong to the body," that would not make it any less a part of the body either. If the whole body were an eye, where would the hearing be? If the whole body were an ear and hearing only, where would the sense of smell be? But as it is, God arranged the members in the body, each one of them, as he chose. If all were a single member, where would the body be? As it is, there are many parts, yet one body.

The eye cannot say to the hand, "I have no need of you," or the head to the feet, "I have no need of you." Oh no, the parts of the body that seem to be weaker are indispensable, and on those parts of the body that we think less honourable we bestow the greater honour, and our unpresentable parts are treated with greater modesty, which our more presentable parts do not require. But God has so composed the body, giving greater honour to the part that lacked it, that there may be no division in the body, but that the members may have the same care for one another. If one member suffers, all suffer together; if one member is honoured, all rejoice together.

Now you are the body of Christ and individually members of it.

Craft: Circular Paper Dolls-

This is a great way to show different people connected and unified in goodwill.

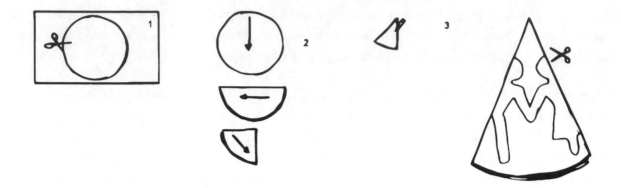

Circular paper dolls instructions

i.   Cut out a large circle from a sheet of paper. You can use the rim of a plate as a template to draw the circle and then cut it out,

ii. Fold the circle in half three times (in half, into quarters, and then into eights). You will get a pie-piece shape.

iii. Draw out two half-figures as shown. In this example, half a man is on the left and half a woman is on the right. It is easier to have the heads pointing in towards the centre of the circle and the feet pointing out towards the perimeter.

iv. Cut out the figures and unfold. You will find 8 figures holding hands to form a complete circle.

Decorate the figures with eyes, nose, mouth, hair, and clothes.

Responsibility Ezekiel 33:1-19

Ezekiel Is Israel's Watchman

The word of the Lord came to Ezekiel: "Son of man, speak to your people and say to them, If I bring the sword upon a land, and the people of the land take a man from among them, and make him their watchman, and if he sees the sword coming upon the land and blows the trumpet and warns the people, then if anyone who hears the sound of the trumpet does not take warning, and the sword comes and takes him away, his blood shall be upon his own head. He heard the sound of the trumpet and did not take warning; his blood shall be upon himself. But if he had taken warning, he would have saved his life. But if the watchman sees the sword coming and does not blow the trumpet, so that the people are not warned, and the sword comes and takes any one of them, that person is taken away in his iniquity, but his blood I will require at the watchman's hand for he was responsible for warning everybody.

Craft: Responsibility Hive Graph-

<u>Materials:</u>

1. *Honeycomb template*
2. *Black markers*
3. *Glue*
4. Scissors
5. Yellow and orange crayons/pencils
6. Black cardboard

Colour beehive honeycomb 'squares' yellow and orange. Cut out and stick to black card. Using a Black marker get children to write (they may need adult help) things they are responsible for. Stick a bee next to their 'hive' and write 'I am being responsible for…'.

Anxiety Matthew 6:25-34

Jesus said; "Therefore I tell you, do not worry about your life, what you will eat or drink; or about your body, what you will wear. Is not life more important than food, and the body more important than clothes? Look at the birds of the air; they do not sow or reap or store away in barns, and yet your heavenly Father feeds them. Are you not much more valuable than they? Who of you by worrying can add a single hour to their life? "And why do you worry about clothes? See how the lilies of the field grow. They do not labour or spin. Yet I tell you that not even Solomon, a great and wealthy king, in all his splendour was dressed like one of these. If that is how God clothes the grass of the field, which is here today and tomorrow is thrown into the fire, will God not provide more for you? So do not worry, saying, 'What shall we eat?' or 'What shall we drink?' or 'What shall we wear?' For those who do not trust run after all these things, and your heavenly Father knows that you need them. But seek first the kingdom of God and God's righteousness, and all these things will be given to you as well. Therefore do not worry about tomorrow, for tomorrow will worry about itself. Each day has enough trouble of its own.

Doves have been a sign of peace for many years. These gentle birds, that mate for life and take care of their young, were used as a peace symbol almost universally from the beginning of recorded history. The birds have always nested in areas close to developments with an unusual trust that they will be unharmed or even protected by humans. Egyptians were the first to record doves used in ceremonies to announce, to the people, the rise of a new pharaoh.

Central Asia also has a legend about two kings heading for war. One king calls for his armor and is told a dove has made a nest in his helmet. The king's mother pleads with her son to leave the mother dove, a gentle bird associated with love, innocence, tenderness and purity, undisturbed.

The king agrees to leave the dove family and heads out to meet his enemy without protection. The second king sees the king without armor and calls for a parley. Both kings lay down their weapons and talk. When the second king hears about the first king's compassion for the mother dove he wonders if he has misjudged the man he thought was a tyrant. Both kings come to an agreement to seek peace for the two kingdoms instead of war. And the dove becomes known throughout the land as a bird of peace. In the Old Testament a dove is released by Noah after the great flood to search for land. It returns with an olive branch to show that the Biblical flood has receded. The dove then symbolized deliverance and God's forgiveness. (Genesis 8:11).

These peaceful birds have woven themselves into histories of cultures all around the world through their gentle presence and fearlessness of humans. Their soulful calls and coos bring many people hope in a chaotic world.

Craft: Dove-

Cut out and fold along dotted lines. Glue wings to top of bird.

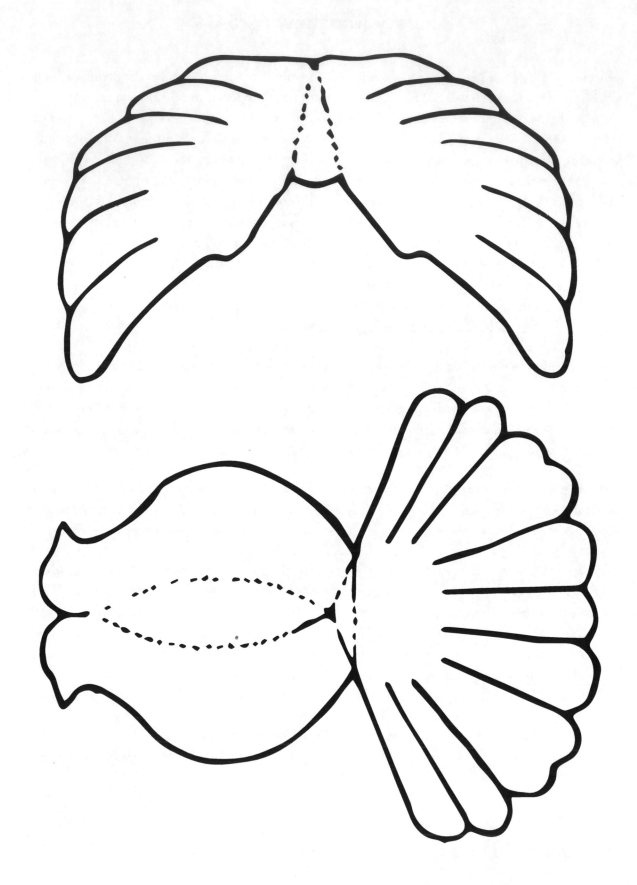

Resting Matthew 11:28-30

Rest is important: for your spiritual health and physical health, and many people today don't appreciate the value of rest or keeping a day for relaxing.

Jesus said; "Come to me, all you who are tired, weary, struggling and burdened, and I will give you rest. Take my yoke upon you and learn from me, for I am gentle and humble in heart, and you will find rest for your souls. For my yoke is easy and my burden is light."

Craft: Cat in a Bed-

Cats are very good at resting. They have their fun, eat and relax. Colour and cut out. Cut a slit above the blanket and slide the cat in from the underside.

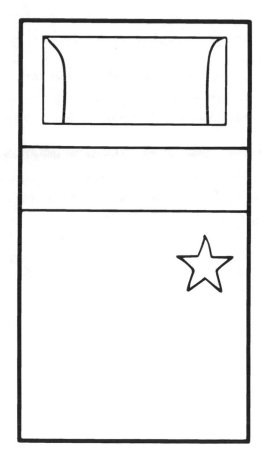

Seeing the bigger picture 1 Corinthians 13:10-13

But when completeness comes, what is in part disappears. When I was a child, I talked like a child, I thought like a child, I reasoned like a child. When I grew up and became a man, I put the ways of childhood behind me. For now we see only a reflection as in a mirror; then we shall see face to face. Now I know in part; then I shall know fully, even as I am fully known. And, when everything is stripped away to the bare basics these three things remain: faith, hope and love.

Craft Activity: Drawing the Picture-

We can not always see everything in its entirety and its important to remember to avoid making judgment calls or high impact decisions without getting all the facts. This craft requires the drawing of an animal from the given description. Remind children it is important to not copy what others are drawing as they may be wrong. This activity will show a variety of images even though they were given access to the same limited information. There is the ability to discuss what other information they may have needed to get an accurate picture.

The [red fox] is typically active at dusk or at night. The diet is extremely broad, and includes small mammals, many invertebrates, and birds, as well as fruit, carrion and items scavenged from dustbins, bird tables and compost heaps.

It is the size of a small dog, it has a large bushy tail, which is often tipped with white. The fur is variable in colour, but is usually reddish-brown to flame-red above and white to black below; it has four lower limbs, and these, like the back of the two pointy ears on its head are often black.

Judging Others Matthew 7:1-5 and Romans 12:16-19

"Judge not, so that you will not judged. For with the judgment you pronounce on others you will be judged by the same measure, and with the measure you use it will be measured to you. Why do you see the tiny speck that is in somebody else's eye, but do not notice the log that is in your own eye? Or how can you say to somebody else, 'Let me take the speck out of your eye,' when there is the log in your own eye? You hypocrite, first take the log out of your own eye, and then you will see clearly to take the speck out of your their eye.

Live in harmony with one another. Do not be haughty, but associate with the lowly. Never be wise in your own sight. Repay no one evil for evil, but give thought to do what is honourable in the sight of all. If possible, so far as it depends on you, live peaceably with all. Beloved, never avenge yourselves, or seeking out ways to get back at others, but leave it to the wrath of God, for it is written, "Vengeance is mine, I will repay, says the Lord."

We have all heard the sayings, "walking a mile in someone else's shoes" or "You can't understand a person until you have walked a mile in their shoes," "Don't judge someone until you've walked a mile in their shoes" and you really cannot. You still see things from your own perspective. It's a reminder that we can NEVER know what it's like to be that person.

When you hear, see or experience other people's lives our mind reacts to try to put ourselves in their shoes and consider how we would deal with it. It's impossible, for us to actually do so from their true perspective. We would hear, see, and experience things differently and our history of life and personal make up affect that.

Let's take the saying literal – if I were to walk in your shoes for a mile my foot maybe larger or smaller, contoured differently with a higher or lower arch. My foot might be wider or narrower. I will NEVER feel what you do! I would feel your shoes through my feet! It would help me understand what it's like to be me wearing your shoes, but it still doesn't mean I know what YOU feel!

Craft Activity: Shoe-

Colour and cut out. Fold on dotted lines and glue tabs, gluing the tabs coloured black so they are not visible.

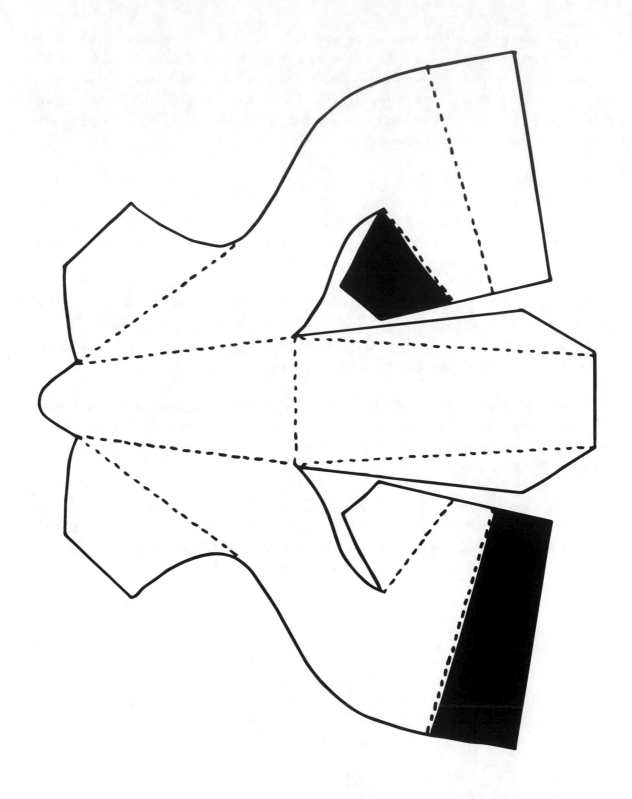

Fruits of the Spirit

This is a series of lessons that moves through the characteristics of the Spirit. These are totally in harmony with the full spiritual intent of God's holy and beneficial law, and every human government would be happy to have citizens exhibiting these traits. Growing in the fruit of the Spirit is expected of those who have decided to turn to God. We are to grow to think and act more like God does, and the fruit of the Spirit help outline this path. Some of the fruits are run together as they are naturally linked or paired and are kept within this broader linkage.

Fruits of the Spirit Galatians 5:22-23

But the fruit of the Spirit is love, joy, peace, forbearance, kindness, goodness, faithfulness, gentleness and self-control.

Love

This love denotes a really undefeatable benevolence and unconquerable goodwill, that always seeks the highest of the other, no matter what s/he does. It is the self-giving love that gives freely without asking anything in return, and does not consider the worth of its object. It describes the unconditional love God has for the world. Paul describes love in 1 Corinthians 13:

Love is patient. Love is kind. Love is not jealous. Love is not pompous, Love is not inflated. Love is not rude. Love does not seek its own interests, it is not quick-tempered, it does not brood over injury, it does not rejoice over wrongdoing but rejoices with the truth. Love bears all things, believes all things, hopes all things, endures all things. And above all, love never fails.

Craft Activity: Heart Mice-

Mice made out of hearts. Print out hearts onto red and pink paper. Cut out and fold large heart in half and fold the dotted lines in at the end of the heart. Stick tabs together. Add details such as eyes and tail.

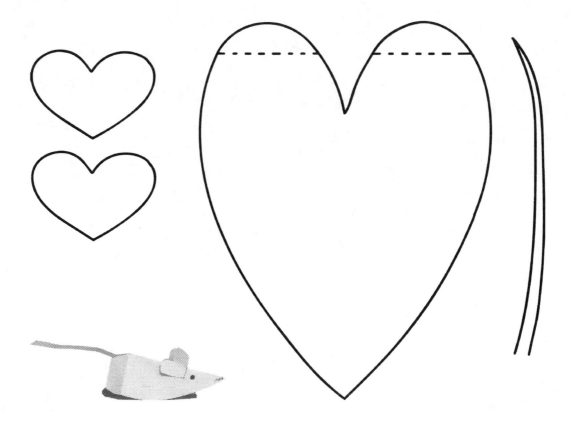

Joy

The joy referred to here is deeper than mere happiness, is rooted in God and comes from him. Since it comes from God, it is more serene and stable than worldly joy, which is merely emotional and lasts only for a time. The fruit of joy is the awareness that God is one's strength and protector.

St. Paul wrote in Philippians 4:4, "Rejoice in the Lord always. I shall say it again: rejoice!"

Peace

Peace is the result of resting in a relationship with God. Peace is more than an absence of conflict. It is the tranquil state of a soul fearing nothing from God and content with its earthly lot, of what so ever sort that is. It is a kind of equilibrium that comes from trusting that everything is in the hands of God.

Craft Activity: Origami Tadpole-

We know that God is in charge so we don't need to worry or be anxious. Tadpoles do not know what is ahead of them, or where the changes in themselves and their lives will lead. But no matter the changes, things work out.

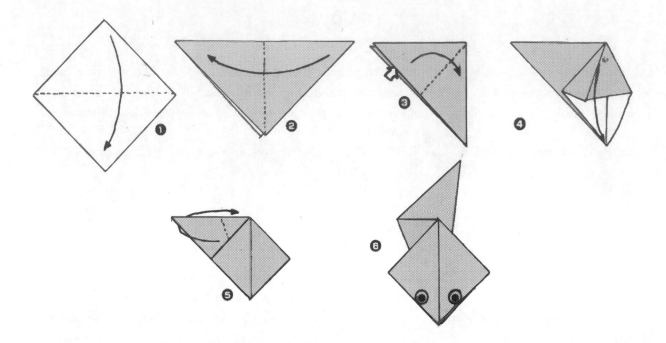

Origami Tadpole instructions

Take a square sheet of paper and position it so it looks like a diamond shape.

    i.   *Fold piece of paper in half.*
    ii.   *Fold in half again.*
    iii.   *Open the arrow part to make space.*
    iv.   *Flatten to triangle.*
    v.   *Fold backward on the dotted line.*

Decorate the tadpole with eyes.

Patience

Generally this word in the Bible referred to a man who could avenge them selves but did not. This word is often used in the Greek Scriptures in reference to God and his attitude to all people.

It describes a person who has the power to exercise revenge but instead exercises restraint.

Exodus 34:6 describes the Lord as "slow to anger and rich in kindness and fidelity."

Patience includes the concepts of forbearance, long-suffering, and the willingness to bear wrongs patiently.

Ask the children about Noah and his family and only fill in the gaps in their version of events as you tell the story of the Flood. The reason for this is you do not want replication in stories as just stories. And, unlike most Biblical passages dealt with in this section, this is a story that many of the children will be able to contribute to. We want them to engage with, and bring alive, our Biblical narrative.

Discuss with the children what it must have been like for all those animals to be stuck on the ark together. Discuss what it must have been like for the family and siblings to be stuck together without a break.

Craft Activity: Noah's Ark.

Imagine being stuck on a boat with lots of animals and only your family for over a month. There would be lots of moments where we would need to use our patience.

Colour in the template. The bottom half of the circle is the water. The top half of the circle is the rainbow. The three shapes are the Ark. Once coloured, cut out and stick the ark pieces together in the middle of the picture.

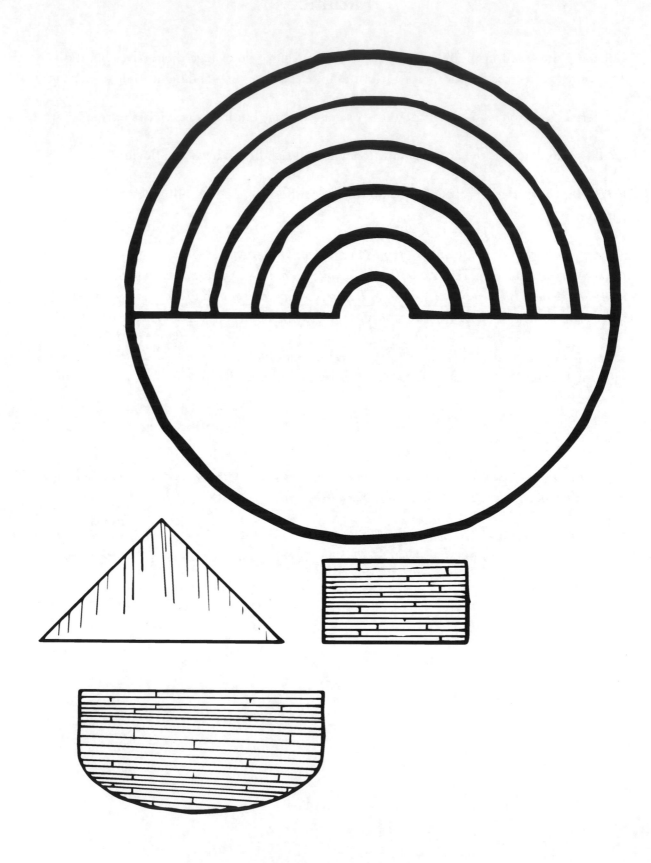

Kindness

Kindness is acting for the good of people regardless of what they do, properly, "useable, i.e. well-fit for use (for what is really needed); kindness that is also serviceable".

Kindness is goodness in action, sweetness of disposition, gentleness in dealing with others, benevolence, kindness, affability. The word describes *the ability to act for the welfare of those taxing your patience.* The Holy Spirit removes abrasive qualities from the character of one under His control.

Kindness is doing something and not expecting anything in return. Kindness is respect and helping others without waiting for someone to help one back. It implies kindness no matter what. We should live "in purity, understanding, patience and kindness; in the Holy Spirit and in sincere love; in truthful speech and in the power of God; with weapons of righteousness in the right hand and in the left".

Goodness

The state or quality of being good

1. Moral excellence; virtue;
2. Kindly feeling, kindness, generosity, joy in being good
3. The best part of anything; Essence; Strength;
4. General character recognized in quality or conduct.

Popular English Bibles translate the single Greek word *chrestotes* into two English words: kindness and goodness. "Wherefore also we pray always for you, that our God would count you worthy of this calling, and fulfill all the good pleasure of his goodness, and the work of faith with power". "For the fruit of the Spirit is in all goodness and righteousness and truth",

Craft Activity: Paper Fan with Polar Bear-

Stay cool and kind, don't be a grumpy bear. Using a piece of A4 paper, using concertina fold make a fan. Unfold slightly and using a crayon draw two eyes, a nose and a mouth. Cut out two bear ear shapes (two half circles) from another piece of white paper and stick on. Refold. Stick the 'handle' into a wooden peg.

Faithfulness

Faithfulness is committing oneself to something or someone, for instance, to one's spouse, to a cause, or to a religion. Being faithful requires personal resolve not to wander away from commitments or promises. It's not always easy to be faithful. Christian faith requires trust in God.

Ephisians 3:16-17: "O Lord, you are my God; I will exalt you, I will praise your name; for you have done wonderful things; your counsels of old are faithfulness and truth". "I pray that out of his glorious riches he may strengthen you with power through his Spirit in your inner being, so that Christ may dwell in your hearts through faith".

The writer of the Letter to the Hebrews describes it this way: "Let us fix our eyes on Jesus, the author and perfecter of our faith, who for the joy set before him endured the cross, scorning its shame, and sat down at the right hand of the throne of God".

Craft Activity: Story and Stones-

Read the story of David the faithful shepherd and make bag with stones. Print and cut out the template of the bag. Fold in half brown cardboard and trace the bag onto it and cut out so that you have two sides of a bag. Staple the sides and bottom shut. Cut out circles of grey felt or card and stick them inside the bag.

Another option would be to get the children to write on some stones the things that help them feel confident, the things they feel good at.

David and Goliath

The Philistines gathered their forces for war. Saul and the Israelites assembled and camped in the Valley of Elah, and drew up their battle line to meet the Philistines. The Philistines occupied one hill, and the Israelites another, with the valley between them.

A champion named Goliath, came out of the Philistine camp. His was a Giant!

Goliath stood and shouted to the ranks of Israel, "Why do you come out and line up for battle? Am I not a Philistine, and are you not the servants of Saul? Choose a man and have him come down to me. If he is able to fight and kill me, we will become your subjects; but if I overcome him and kill him, you will become our subjects and serve us." Then the Philistine said, "This day I defy the armies of Israel! Give me a man and let us fight each other." On hearing the Philistine's words, Saul and all the Israelites were dismayed and terrified.

There was a young man named David. David's older brothers followed Saul, but David went back and forth from Saul to tend his father's sheep at Bethlehem.

One day his father said; "Take this roasted grain and these ten loaves of bread for your brothers and hurry to their camp. Take along these ten cheeses to the commander of their unit. See how your brothers are and bring back some assurance from them. They are with Saul and all the men of Israel in the Valley of Elah, fighting against the Philistines."

Early in the morning David left the flock in the care of a shepherd, loaded up and set out. He reached the camp as the army was going out to its battle positions, shouting the war cry. Israel and the Philistines were drawing up their lines facing each other. David left his things with the keeper of supplies, ran to the battle lines and asked his brothers how they were. As he was talking with them, Goliath stepped out from his lines and shouted and David heard it. Whenever the Israelites saw the man, they all fled from him in great fear.

David asked the men standing near him, "What will be done for the man who kills this Philistine and removes this disgrace from Israel? Who is this that he should defy the armies of the living God?"

The Israelites replied; "Do you see how this man keeps coming out? He comes out to defy Israel. The king will give great wealth to the man who kills him. He will also give him his daughter in marriage and will exempt his family from taxes in Israel."

What David said was overheard and reported to Saul, and Saul sent for him.

David said to Saul, "Let no one lose heart on account of this Philistine; your servant will go and fight him."

Saul replied, "You are not able to go out against this Philistine and fight him; you are only a young man, and he has been a warrior from his youth."

But David said to Saul, "Your servant has been keeping his father's sheep. When a lion or a bear came and carried off a sheep from the flock, I went after it, struck it and rescued the sheep from its mouth. When it turned on me, I seized it by its hair, struck it and killed it. Your servant has killed both the lion and the bear; Goliath will be like one of them, because he has defied the armies of the living God. The Lord who rescued me from the paw of the lion and the paw of the bear will rescue me from the hand of this Philistine."

Saul said to David, "Go, and the Lord be with you."

Then Saul dressed David in his own tunic. He put a coat of armour on him and a bronze helmet on his head. David fastened on his sword over the tunic and tried walking around, because he was not used to them.

"I cannot go in these," he said to Saul, "because I am not used to them." So he took them off. Then he took his staff in his hand, chose five smooth stones from the stream, put them in the pouch of his shepherd's bag and, with his sling in his hand, approached the Philistine.

Meanwhile, the Philistine, with his shield bearer in front of him, kept coming closer to David. He looked David over and saw that he was little more than a boy, glowing with health and handsome, and he despised him. He said to David, "Am I a dog, that you come at me with sticks?" And the Philistine cursed David by his gods. "Come here," he said, "and I'll give your flesh to the birds and the wild animals!"

David said to the Philistine, "You come against me with sword and spear and javelin, but I come against you in the name of the Lord Almighty, the God of the armies of Israel, whom you have defied. This day the Lord will deliver you into my hands, and I'll strike you down and cut off your head. This very day I will give the carcasses of the Philistine army to the birds and the wild animals, and the whole world will know that there is a God in Israel. All those gathered here will know that it is not by sword or spear that the Lord saves; for the battle is the Lord's, and he will give all of you into our hands."

As the Philistine moved closer to attack him, David ran quickly toward the battle line to meet him. Reaching into his bag and taking out a stone, he slung it and struck the Philistine on the forehead. The stone sank into his forehead, and he fell facedown on the ground.

So David triumphed over the Philistine with a sling and a stone; without a sword in his hand he struck down the Philistine and killed him. David ran and stood over him. He took hold of the Philistine's sword and drew it from the sheath. After he killed him, he cut off his head with the sword.

Gentleness

Gentleness is also commonly known as meekness. It is "a disposition that is even-tempered, tranquil, balanced in spirit, unpretentious, and that has the passions under control. The word is best translated; 'meekness,' not as an indication of weakness, but of power and strength under control. The person who possesses this quality pardons injuries, corrects faults, and rules his own spirit well".

Galatians 6:1 "Brothers and sisters, if someone is caught in a sin, in falling short of expectations, you who live by the Spirit should restore that person gently. But watch yourselves, or you also may be tempted".

Ephesians 4:2 "Be completely humble and gentle; be patient, bearing with one another in love".

Craft Activity: Reindeer Antlers-

Colour and cut out. Stick ears and antlers to the strip that runs across the forehead. Using a spare sheet of paper run a strip around the back of the head and join up to the front section.

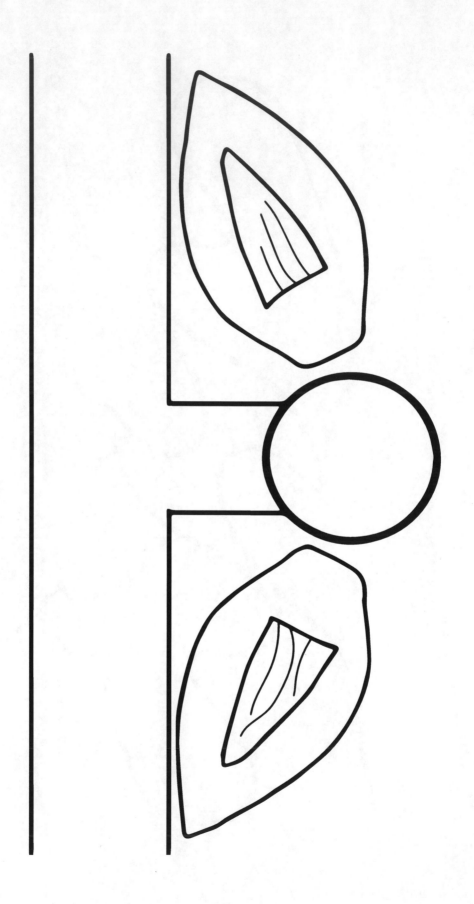

Self-control

The Greek word used in Galatians 5:23 is "egkrateia", meaning "strong, having mastery, able to control one's thoughts and actions."

2 Peter 1:5-7 "...make every effort to add to your faith goodness; and to goodness, knowledge; and to knowledge, self-control; and to self-control, perseverance; and to perseverance, godliness; and to godliness, mutual affection; and to mutual affection, love".

Jesus maintained self-control and so can we (Hebrew 4:12-16)

The word of God is indeed living and active. It is sharper than any two-edged sword piercing to the division of soul and of spirit, of joints and of marrow, and so sharp it even discerns the thoughts and intentions of the heart. No person, no creature, is hidden from God's sight. Instead all are naked and exposed to the eyes of him to whom we must give account.

Since then we have a great high priest, Jesus, who has passed through the heavens, the Son of God, let us hold fast our confession. For we can rest easily knowing that we do not have a high priest who is unable to sympathize with our weaknesses, but one who in every respect has been tempted as we are, yet without sin. Jesus was tempted but he never sinned: he never fell short of the expectations required to be the Messiah. He was not mean to those who were mean to him, he never stole and he never lied. Jesus not only maintained self-control to keep himself from doing wrong things. He had so much self-control that He was always able to the right things and all that was required. Let us then with confidence draw near to the throne of grace, that we may receive mercy and find grace to help in times of need and when we struggle with our self-control.

Craft Activity: Traffic Light-

Print out and children colour in. The reason for a traffic light is that it is an everyday example of where we need to maintain self-control.

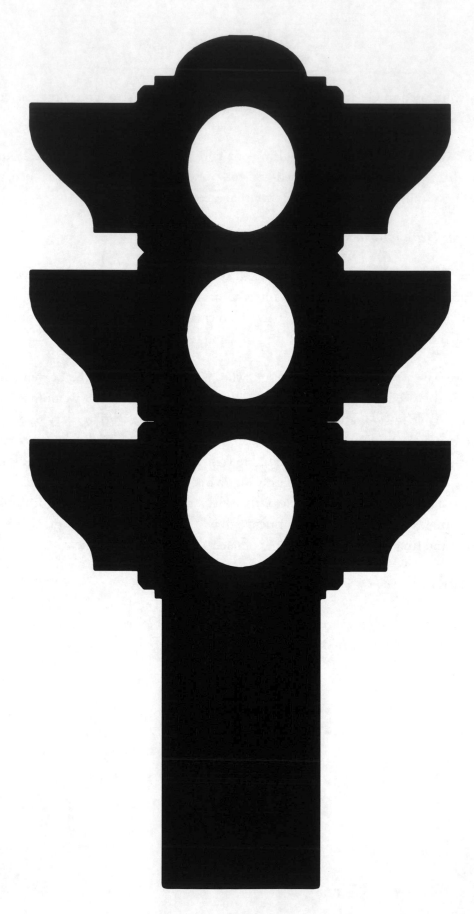

Being Kind

This is a series of lessons that walk children through different aspects of being kind. We live in a world that, much of the time, focuses on the negative. These lessons are designed to encourage children to choose to focus on the abundant good that is all around them.

Acts of Kindness Luke 5:17-26

Jesus Forgives and Heals a Paralysed Man

One day Jesus was teaching, and Pharisees and teachers of the law were sitting there. They had come from every village of Galilee and from Judea and Jerusalem. Jesus had the power to heal the sick. Some men came carrying a paralysed man on a mat and tried to take him into the house to lay him before Jesus. But because the crowed was so big they could not find a way to do so. They went up on the roof and lowered him on his mat through the tiles into the middle of the crowd, right in front of Jesus.

When Jesus saw their faith, he said, "Friend, your sins are forgiven."

The Pharisees and the teachers of the law began thinking to themselves, "Who is this fellow who speaks blasphemy? Who can forgive sins but God alone?"

Jesus knew what they were thinking and asked, "Why are you thinking these things in your hearts? Which is easier: to say, 'Your sins are forgiven,' or to say, 'Get up and walk'? But I want you to know that the Son of Man has authority on earth to forgive sins." So he said to the paralysed man, "I tell you, get up, take your mat and go home." Immediately he stood up in front of them, took what he had been lying on and went home praising God. Everyone was amazed and gave praise to God. They were filled with awe and said; "We have seen remarkable things today."

Key concepts

Four friends brought their paralyzed friend to see Jesus so he could be healed. Jesus healed the man to bring praise to God, not Himself. When we are kind, we should do it for others not ourselves.

Craft Activity: Plant Pot-

Friendships only grow when we nourish them with kindness. This is like a plant being nourished by water. Print out the plant pot. Children colour in and decorate their pot. Then, using coloured paper (or cupcake patty pans) make flowers and stick above pot. Using crayons, have the children draw in stems and leaves.

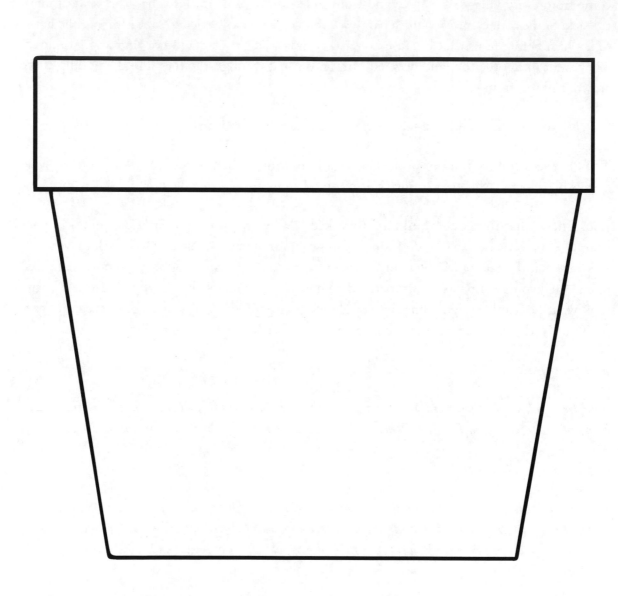

Love your Enemies Luke 6:27-36

Jesus said; "But to you who are listening I say: Love your enemies, do good to those who hate you, bless those who curse you, pray for those who mistreat you. If someone slaps you on one cheek, turn to them your other cheek also. If someone takes your coat, do not withhold your shirt from them but hand it over also. Give to everyone who asks you, and if anyone takes what belongs to you, do not demand it back. Do to others as you would have them do to you.

"If you love those who love you, what credit is that to you? Even sinners love those who love them. And if you do good to those who are good to you, what credit is that to you? Even sinners do that. And if you lend to those from whom you expect repayment, what credit is that to you? Even sinners lend to sinners, expecting to be repaid in full. But love your enemies, do good to them, and lend to them without expecting to get anything back. Then your reward will be great, and you will be children of the Most High, because he is kind to the ungrateful and wicked. Be merciful, just as your Father is merciful.

Questions for discussion

1. Is it easy to be kind? If so, when?
2. When are you tempted to be unkind?

Key concepts

Jesus talked about a common saying, "Love your neighbour and hate your enemy." He said that He didn't agree. Instead, Jesus encouraged His followers to love their enemies and pray for those who were unkind to them. The Bible says that Jesus showed His love for us by "laying down his life"' (dying on the cross for our sins). 1 John 3:16-18 also tells us that the best way to show we have God's love in our hearts is to share what we have with those who need it.

Craft Activity: Cat and Mouse Finger Puppets.

Colour and cut out the bits to make the mouse and cat. Roll the body to form a cone and stick the tab edge underneath the body. Stick head and tail to body.

Showing Kindness Luke 10:25-37

On one occasion an expert in the law stood up to test Jesus. "Teacher," he asked, "what must I do to inherit eternal life?" "What is written in the Law?" he replied. "How do you read it?"

He answered, "'Love the Lord your God with all your heart and with all your soul and with all your strength and with all your mind'; and, 'Love your neighbour as yourself.'"

"You have answered correctly," Jesus replied. "Do this and you will live." But he wanted to justify himself, so he asked Jesus, "And who is my neighbour?"

In reply Jesus told a story: "A man was going down from Jerusalem to Jericho, when he was attacked by nasty robbers. They stripped him of his clothes, beat him and went away, leaving him half dead. A priest happened to be going down the same road, and when he saw the man, he passed by on the other side. Then a Levite came by and when he came to the place and saw the man, he too passed by on the other side. But a Samaritan, as he travelled, came where the man was; and when he saw him, he took pity on him. He went to him and bandaged his wounds, pouring on oil and wine. Then he put the man on his own donkey, brought him to an inn and took care of him. The next day he gave some money to the innkeeper. 'Look after him,' he said, 'and when I return, I will reimburse you for any extra expense you may have.'

"Which of these three do you think was a neighbour to the man who fell into the hands of robbers?"

The expert in the law replied, "The one who had mercy on him."

Jesus told him, "Go and do likewise."

Key concepts

Jesus told this story to help people understand that it is important to show love to everyone. If we only show compassion to some people, we are not truly sharing God's love with others. The Samaritan in the story showed love to the injured man because he had pity on him and cared for him. The Levite and the priest, although they were considered to be spiritual leaders, did not show love to the injured man. Jesus ended the story by saying, "Go and do likewise." We show true compassion and kindness when we go out of our way to help someone else, even with people we don't even know.

Craft Activity: Band-Aids and Box.

Colour in band-Aids. Cut out box and, if children would like, have them decorate it. Fold on dotted lines. Stick side and bottom tabs together and insert band-Aids into box.

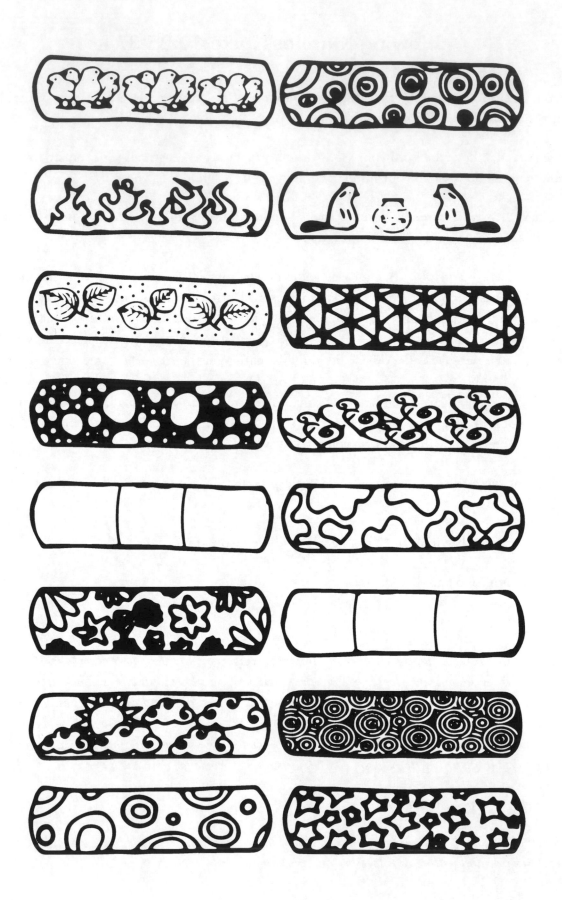

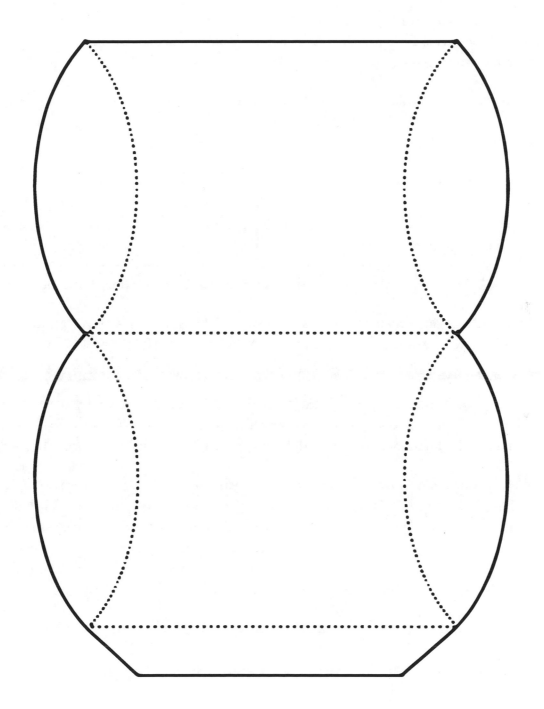

Responding to Kindness 1 Samuel
25:2-42 and Psalm 94:1-2.

Once, there was a very wealthy man named Nabal. He had a thousand goats and three thousand sheep, which he was shearing. Nabal's wife was Abigail. She was an intelligent and beautiful woman, but her husband was surly and mean in his dealings.

While David was in the wilderness, he heard that Nabal was shearing sheep. So he sent ten young men and said to them, "Go up to Nabal at Carmel and greet him in my name. Say to him: 'Long life to you! Good health to you and your household! And good health to all that is yours!

"'Now I hear that it is sheep-shearing time. When your shepherds were with us, we did not mistreat them, and the whole time they were at Carmel nothing of theirs was missing. Ask your own servants and they will tell you. Therefore be favorable toward my men, since we come at a festive time. Please give your servants and your son David whatever you can find for them.'"

When David's men arrived, they gave Nabal this message in David's name. Then they waited.

Nabal answered David's servants, "Who is this David? Who is this son of Jesse? Many servants are breaking away from their masters these days. Why should I take my bread and water, and the meat I have slaughtered for my shearers, and give it to men coming from who knows where?"

David's men turned around and went back. When they arrived, they reported every word. David said to his men, "Each of you strap on your sword!" So they did, and David strapped his on as well. About four hundred men went up with David, while two hundred stayed with the supplies.

One of the servants told Abigail; "David sent messengers from the wilderness to give our master his greetings, but he hurled insults at them. Yet these men were very good to us. They did not mistreat us, and the whole time we were out in the fields near them nothing was missing. Night and day they were a wall around us the whole time we were herding our sheep near them. Now think it over and see what you can do, because disaster is hanging over our master and his whole household. He is such a wicked man that no one can talk to him."

Abigail acted quickly. She took two hundred loaves of bread, two skins of wine, five dressed sheep, 27kg of roasted grain, a hundred cakes of raisins and two hundred cakes of pressed figs, and loaded them on donkeys. Then she told her servants, "Go on ahead; I'll follow you." But she did not tell her husband Nabal.

As she came riding her donkey into a mountain ravine, there were David and his men descending toward her, and she met them. David had just said, "It's been useless—all my watching over this fellow's property in the wilderness so that nothing of his was missing. He has paid me back evil for good. May God deal with David, be it ever so severely, if by morning I leave alive one male of all who belong to him!"

When Abigail saw David, she quickly got off her donkey and bowed down before David with her face to the ground. She fell at his feet and said: "Pardon your servant, my lord, and let me speak to you; hear what your servant has to say. Please pay no attention, my lord, to that wicked man Nabal. He is just like his name—his name means Fool, and folly goes with him. And as for me, your servant, I did not see the men my lord sent. And now, my lord, as surely as the Lord your God lives and as you live, since the Lord has kept you from bloodshed and from avenging yourself with your own hands, may your enemies and all who are intent on harming my lord be like Nabal. And let this gift, which your servant has brought to my lord, be given to the men who follow you".

David said to Abigail, "Praise be to the Lord, the God of Israel, who has sent you today to meet me. May you be blessed for your good judgment and for keeping me from bloodshed this day and from avenging myself with my own hands. Otherwise, as surely as the Lord, the God of Israel, lives, who has kept me from harming you, if you had not come quickly to meet me, not one male belonging to Nabal would have been left alive by daybreak."

Then David accepted from her hand what she had brought him and said, "Go home in peace. I have heard your words and granted your request."

Questions for discussion

Have you ever been kind to someone and they were mean in return?

How did that make you feel?

In this story, what did David do that was kind to Nabal?

What did Nabal do when David asked him for a favour?

What was David going to do?

What did Abigail do?

When someone is unkind to us, what are we to do?

Key concepts

David and his men had been very kind to Nabal's men, but when David asked Nabal for a favour, he refused to return David's kindness. This made David angry, and he was going to fight Nabal. Fortunately, Nabal's wife Abigail became aware of the situation and went to ask David to forgive her husband for his unkindness. Although David knew that it was wrong to take revenge, he was still planning to do so. In the end, David thanked Abigail for preventing him from fighting Nabal.

When we are tempted to pay someone back for their unkindness to us, we need to remember David and Nabal. It is not our job to get back at someone for their actions. We need to focus on being nicer and better and kinder people, and mending hurt, especially emotional hurt. We sometimes represent emotional hurt by the statement they break our heart

Craft Activity: Broken Heart-

Print out broken hearts. Children cut them and paste them together onto a nice piece of card stock.

Jesus is kind to Children Mark 10:13-16.

People were bringing little children to Jesus for him to place his hands on them, but the disciples rebuked them. When Jesus saw this, he was indignant. He said to them, "Let the little children come to me, and do not hinder them, for the kingdom of God belongs to such as these. Truly I tell you, anyone who will not receive the kingdom of God like a little child will never enter it." And he took the children in his arms, placed his hands on them and blessed them.

Questions for discussion

1. *What does it mean to hurt someone's feelings?*
2. *How do people hurt your feelings?*
3. *Did the disciples consider the feelings of the little children?*
4. *What did Jesus do for the children?*
5. *How can we bless other people?*
6. *How can we show others that we think they are valuable?*

Key concepts

Ignoring others, leaving them out or telling them to go away is unkind and will likely hurt their feelings. We can be a blessing to others by treating them as though they are valuable. This is what Jesus did when the parents brought their children to Him.

Craft Activity: Bees-

For this craft you will need blue cardstock, yellow paint, black crayon and tissues. Get children to make a fist. Paint the 'pinky' side of their fist in yellow and press firmly onto blue cardstock. Draw antenna from top, and black stripes over the body; adding a black tip at the base for the sting. Cut out wings from a tissue and stick to the sides of the bee.

Be kind to All Numbers 22:21-39

Balaam's Donkey

Balaam got up in the morning, saddled his donkey and went with the Moabite officials. But God was very angry when he went, and an angel stood in the road to stop him. Balaam was riding on his donkey, and his two servants were with him. When the donkey saw the angel standing in the road with a drawn sword in his hand, it turned off the road into a field. Balaam beat it to get it back on the road.

Then the angel stood in a narrow path through the vineyards, with walls on both sides. When the donkey saw the angel, it pressed close to the wall, crushing Balaam's foot against it. So he beat the donkey again.

Then the angel moved on ahead and stood in a narrow place where there was no room to turn, either to the right or to the left. When the donkey saw the angel, it lay down under Balaam, and he was angry and beat it with his staff. Then the angel opened the donkey's mouth, and it said to Balaam, "What have I done to you to make you beat me these three times?"

Balaam answered the donkey, "You have made a fool of me! If only I had a sword in my hand, I would kill you right now."

The donkey said to Balaam, "Am I not your own donkey, which you have always ridden, to this day? Have I been in the habit of doing this to you?"

"No," he said.

Then the angel opened Balaam's eyes, and he saw the angel standing in the road with his sword drawn. So he bowed low and fell facedown.

The angel asked him, "Why have you beaten your donkey these three times? I have come here to oppose you because your path is a reckless one before me. The donkey saw me and turned away from me these three times. If it had not turned away, I would certainly have killed you by now, but I would have spared it."

Balaam said to the angel, "I have done the wrong thing. I did not realize you were standing in the road to oppose me. Now if you are displeased, I will go back."

The angel said to Balaam, "Go with the men, but speak only what I tell you." So Balaam went and did as he was told.

Key concepts

Proverbs 12:10

A righteous man has regard for the life of his animal, But even the compassion of the wicked is cruel.

Craft activity: Paper Bear and Tiger-

Print onto cardboard. Children colour their animals in (remind them that they can use any colour they like) and cut out. Fold along dotted lines on the body and along dotted lines to form the neck.

TIGER

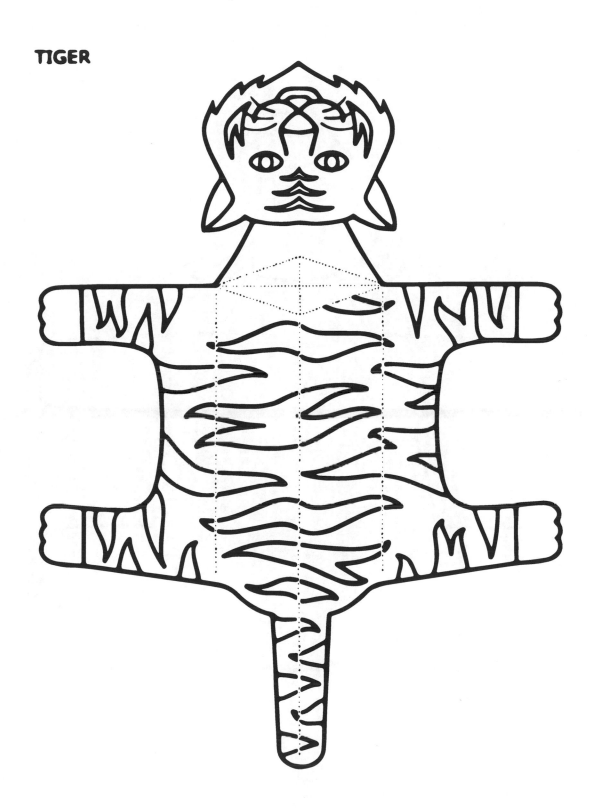

BEAR

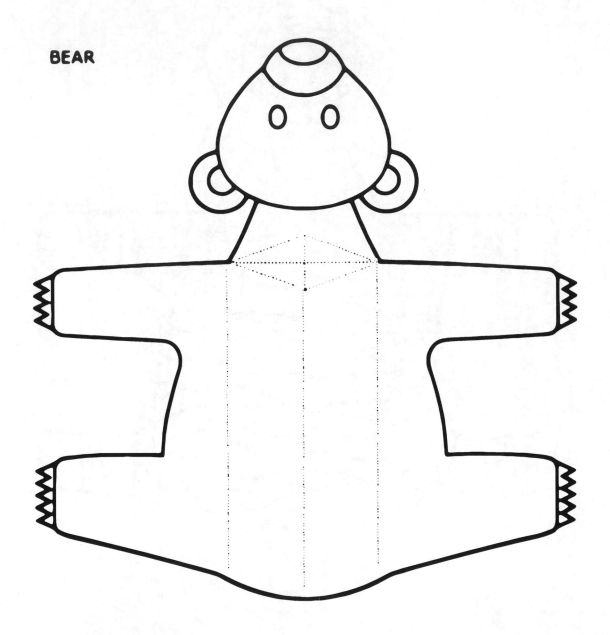

Generosity

This is a series of lessons that focus on generosity and the different ways we can give. It is a set of four lessons and was designed to be 'gap cover' between a set series finishing and the end of a term or before beginning Advent material.

Generosity is the virtue of not being tied down by concerns about one's possessions. Generosity leads to charity and forgiveness.

It is sometimes used in the meaning of charity (the virtue of giving without expecting anything in return. It can involve offering time, assets or talents to aid someone in need).

Generosity can be spending time, money, or labor for others without being rewarded in return.

Although the term generosity often goes hand-in-hand with charity, many people in the public's eye want recognition for their good deeds. Donations are needed to support organizations and committees, however, generosity should not be limited to times of great need such as natural disasters and extreme situations.

Generosity is not solely based on one's economic status, but instead, includes the individual's pure intentions of looking out for society's common good and giving from the heart. Generosity should reflect the individual's passion to help others.

Bible Stories Related to Generosity

1. Jesus feeds the 5000 (the boy who shared his lunch) – Mattew14:14-21; Mark 6: 34-44; Luke 9:10-17 and John 6:1-11
2. Elijah and the Widow at Zarephath – I Kings 17:7-16 (Key verses: 13 &15)
3. Elijah and the Shunammite couple – II Kings 4:8-10 (Key verse 10)
4. Dorcas (Tabitha) – Acts 9:36-42 (Key Verse: 36)

Jesus feeds the 5000 Mark 6:34-44

When Jesus landed and saw a large crowd, he had compassion on them, because they were like sheep without a shepherd. So he began teaching them many things.

By this time it was late in the day, so his disciples came to him. "This is a remote place," they said, "and it's already very late. **36** Send the people away so that they can go to the surrounding countryside and villages and buy themselves something to eat."

But he answered, "You give them something to eat."

They said to him, "That would take more than half a year's wages! Are we to go and spend that much on bread and give it to them to eat?"

"How many loaves do you have?" he asked. "Go and see."

When they found out, they said, "Five—and two fish."

Then Jesus directed them to have all the people sit down in groups on the green grass. So they sat down in groups of hundreds and fifties. Taking the five loaves and the two fish and looking up to heaven, he gave thanks and broke the loaves. Then he gave them to his disciples to distribute to the people. He also divided the two fish among them all. They all ate and were satisfied, and the disciples picked up twelve basketfuls of broken pieces of bread and fish.

Craft Activity: Making a Lunchbox-

<u>Materials</u>:

1. *Lunchbox template*
2. *Patterened paper or material for the lunchbox straps and Name plate*
3. *Glue*
4. Scissors
5. Crayons/pencils for colouring the lunchbox in

Print out lunchbox template. Using decorative paper cut four slivers to make the straps and one to make the nameplate. You could even use sticker nametags for the lunchbox.

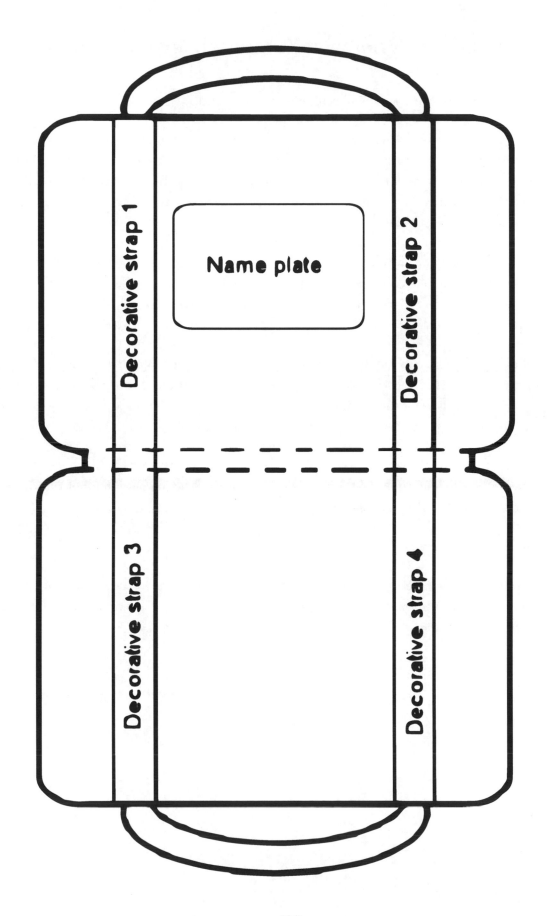

Name plate

Decorative strap 1

Decorative strap 2

Decorative strap 3

Decorative strap 4

Elijah and the Widow at Zarephath 1 Kings 17:7-16

The brook dried up because there had been no rain in the land.

Then the Lord said to Elijah: "Go at once to Zarephath in the region of Sidon and stay there. I have directed a widow there to supply you with food." So he went to Zarephath. When he came to the town gate, a widow was there gathering sticks. He called to her and asked, "Would you bring me a little water in a jar so I may have a drink?" As she was going to get it, he called, "And bring me, please, a piece of bread."

"As surely as the Lord your God lives," she replied, "I don't have any bread—only a handful of flour in a jar and a little olive oil in a jug. I am gathering a few sticks to take home and make a meal for myself and my son, that we may eat it—and after that, will probably die as we will have nothing left to eat."

Elijah said to her, "Don't be afraid. Go home and do as you have said. But first make a small loaf of bread for me from what you have and bring it to me, and then make something for yourself and your son. For this is what the Lord, the God of Israel, says: 'The jar of flour will not be used up and the jug of oil will not run dry until the day the Lord sends rain on the land.'"

She went away and did as Elijah had told her. So there was food every day for Elijah and for the woman and her family. For the jar of flour was not used up and the jug of oil did not run dry, in keeping with the word of the Lord spoken by Elijah.

Craft Activity: Basket of Bread and Croissant-

To make the baskets fold paper plates into thirds making a cone shape. Fold up the bottom pointed end of the cone 7 centimetres from the bottom, and then fold down the end so that it is inside the cone shape making the basket shape

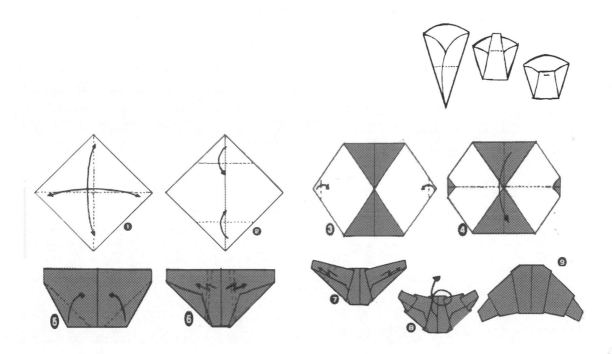

Origami Croissant instructions

Take a square sheet of paper and position it so it looks like a diamond shape.

    i.   *Fold piece of paper in the dotted lines to make creases and fold back.*
    ii.   *Fold the top and bottom corners to meet the centre line.*
    iii.   *Fold left and right corners to the dotted line.*
    iv.   *Fold in half.*
    v.   *Fold in the dotted line.*
    vi.   *Step fold in the dotted line.*
    vii. *Step fold in the dotted line.*
    viii. *Turn over.*

Place croissant into basket

Elisha and the Shunammite couple II Kings 4:8-10

One day a man named Elisha went to Shunem. And a well-to-do woman was there, who urged him to stay for a meal. So whenever he came by, he stopped there to eat. She said to her husband, "I know that this man who often comes our way is a holy man of God. Let's make a small room on the roof and put in it a bed and a table, a chair and a lamp for him. Then he can stay there whenever he comes to us."

One day when Elisha came, he went up to his room and lay down there. He said to his servant Gehazi, "Call the Shunammite." So he called her, and she stood before him. Elisha said to him, "Tell her, 'You have gone to all this trouble for us. Now what can be done for you? Can we speak on your behalf to the king or the commander of the army?'"

She replied, "I have a home among my own people."

"What can be done for her?" Elisha asked.

Gehazi said, "She has no son, and her husband is old."

Then Elisha said, "Call her." So he called her, and she stood in the doorway. "About this time next year," Elisha said, "you will hold a son in your arms."

"No, my lord!" she objected. "Please, man of God, don't mislead your servant!"

But the woman became pregnant, and the next year about that same time she gave birth to a son, just as Elisha had told her.

Craft Activity: Paper Cup with a Slice of Lemon-

When people stay in a hotel, they are often greeted with a smile and a cup of a refreshing drink. Children will want vibrant scrapbooking paper to make the cup. Children will need a slice of lemon. They cut it in half and paste one side to the other.

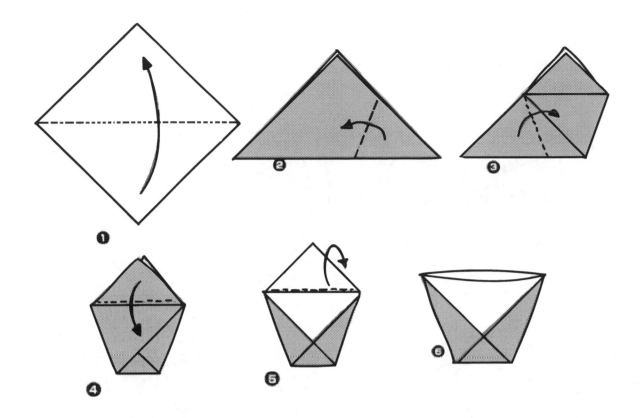

Origami Cup instructions

Take a square sheet of paper and position it so it looks like a diamond shape.

- i.   *Fold piece of paper in the dotted lines to make crease.*
- ii. *Fold in the dotted line.*
- iii. *Fold in the dotted line.*
- iv. *Fold in the dotted line.*
- v.   *Fold backward in the dotted line.*
- vi. *Finished.*

Place slice of lemon onto rim of cup

Dorcas (Tabitha) Acts of the Apostles 9:36-42

Now there was in Joppa a friend of Jesus named Tabitha. She was full of good works and acts of charity. In those days she became ill and died, and when they had washed her, they laid her in an upper room. Since Lydda was near Joppa, the other friends of Jesus, hearing that one of their leaders named Peter was there, sent two men to him, urging him, "Please come to us without delay."

So Peter rose and went with them. And when he arrived, they took him to the upper room. All the widows stood beside him weeping and showing tunics and other garments that Tabitha made while she was with them. But Peter put them all outside, and knelt down and prayed; and turning to the body he said, "Tabitha, arise." And she opened her eyes, and when she saw Peter she sat up. And he gave her his hand and raised her up. Then calling the saints and widows, he presented her alive. And it became known throughout all Joppa, and many believed in the Lord.

Craft Activity: Tabitha T-Shirt-

For this craft you will need lots of small pieces of fabric.

Print out and give to each student a copy of the t-shirt and get students to 'make' a t-shirt by sticking the bits of fabric on to cover the entire picture.

The Whole Armour of God

This is a series of lessons that focus on the armour of God. It is a set of lessons that reminds children of the importance for standing firm in, and up for, what they believe in.

Ephesians 6:10-20

Every day we are faced with challenges. Every moment of every day we are confronted with decisions. It's a bit like being in an army and ready for a battle. Sometimes everything is fine and simple. But then, all of a sudden, something might happen, something that needs us to make a decision. These decisions may even impact on other people and we need to be ready for these moments. It might be someone asking us to put the rubbish outside. It might be seeing our friends about to do the wrong thing.

If we want to be the best we can be, then our decisions need to be the best decisions that we can make. The Bible talks about God's people needing to be ready to do what is right and stand strong in their beliefs.

This passage should be read out each week. Ask students what bits have been done already and what is left.

Finally, be strong in the Lord and in the strength of his power. Put on the whole armour of God, so that you may be able to stand against the wiles of the devil. For our struggle is not against enemies of blood and flesh, but against the rulers, against the authorities, against the cosmic powers of this present darkness, against the spiritual forces of evil in the heavenly places. Therefore take up the whole armour of God, so that you may be able to withstand on that evil day, and having done everything, to stand firm. Stand therefore, and fasten the belt of truth around your waist, and put on the breastplate of righteousness. As shoes for your feet put on whatever will make you ready to proclaim the gospel of peace. With all of these, take the shield of faith, with which you will be able to quench all the flaming arrows of the evil one. Take the helmet of salvation, and the sword of the Spirit, which is the word of God.

Pray in the Spirit at all times in every prayer and supplication. To that end keep alert and always persevere in supplication for all the saints. Pray also for me, so that when I speak, a message may be given to me to make known with boldness the mystery of the gospel, for which I am an ambassador in chains. Pray that I may declare it boldly, as I must speak.

Helmet Of Salvation

When a soldier suited up for battle, the helmet was the last piece of armour to be put on. It was the final act of readiness in preparation for combat. A helmet was vital for survival, protecting the brain, the command station for the rest of the body. If your head gets badly damaged, the rest of the armour is useless. We need to use our heads when we think about how to respond.

1. Colour and cut out the templates.
2. Glue on the straps that will wrap around the head onto the main part of the helmet and glue to size.
3. Next fold the tip of the side pieces. Glue them onto the main part of the helmet (right next to were you glued the straps on).
4. Glue the nasal guard onto the main part of the helmet. Do this by adding a small amount of glue at first to the back of the nosepiece. Have the child place the main part of the helmet on their face (in the position it will go), then centre the nasal guard and stick it onto the helmet. Add more glue if necessary.
5. Add feathers to crest for further fun and creativity.

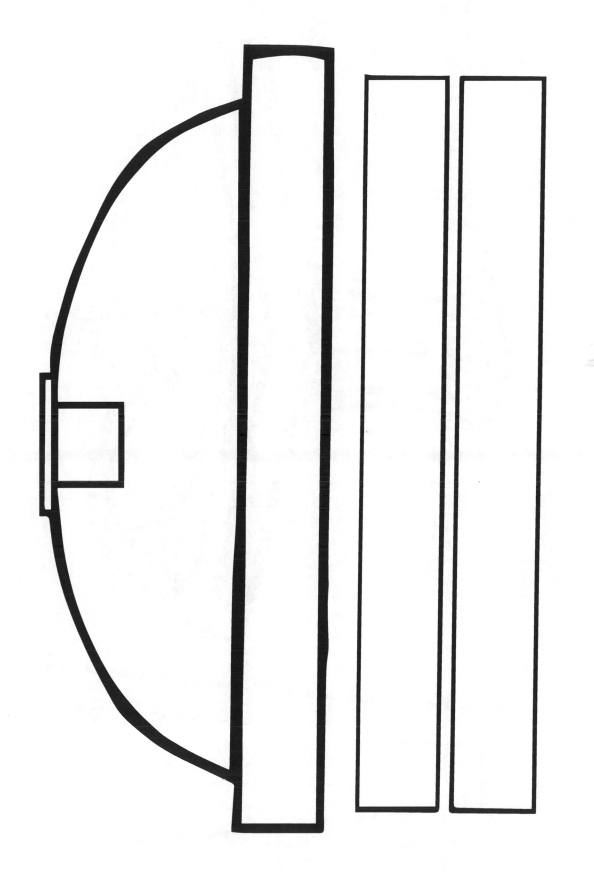

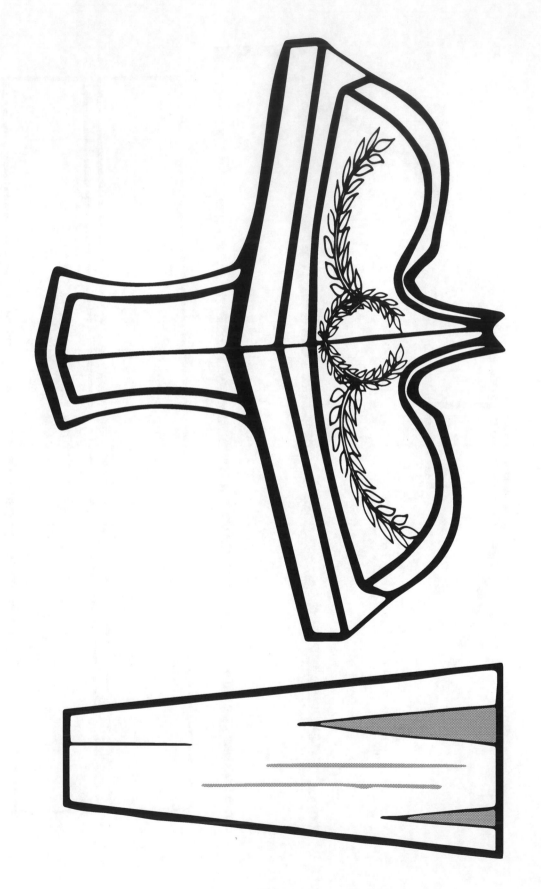

148

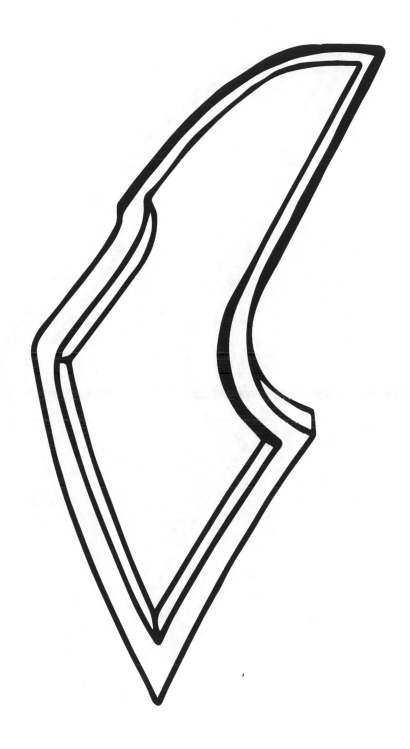

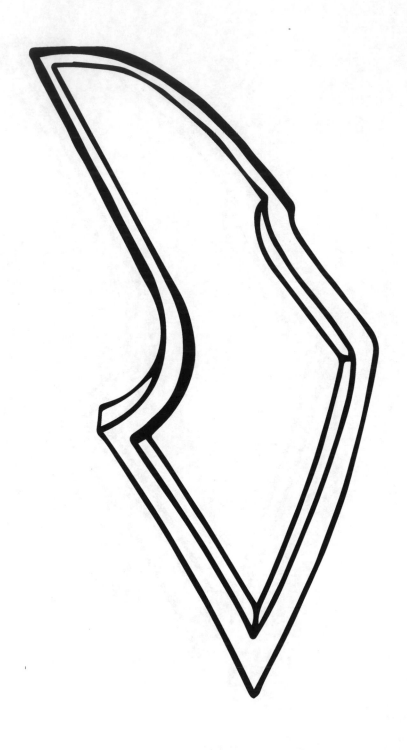

Sword Of The Spirit

Swords are both offensive and defensive weapons. Soldiers or warriors used them to protect from harm or to attack the enemy. In both cases it was necessary for a soldier to get proper training on how to use the sword. We must also make sure we learn and study to know how to best act, behave and respond.

1. Each child will need two copies of the sword. Colour and cut out.
2. Glue each piece of the sword to either poster board, construction paper or onto cardboard.
3. After the glue dries cut both sides out.
4. Glue strips of brown construction paper onto the grip in different spacings and angles. Then cut off any overhang. Or, if working with smaller children simply colour handle in brown.
5. 5 Glue both pieces of the sword together.
6. Finally add glitter glue to the centre of the pommel, a sticker or a large oval jewel.

Shield Of Faith

The Roman shield of the time was called a *scutum*. This type of shield was as large as a door and covered the soldier entirely. The shield could also be used to push opponents. When fighting as a group, a phalanx of soldiers could position their shields so as to form an enclosure around their group, called a *tortoise*. When we see others trying to do the right thing, we also need to join with them to help and support them to be their best too.

1. Print out and glue larger shield template to a piece of cardboard.
2. Cut up the smaller shield template into four individual parts on Different styled sheets of scrapbooking paper.
3. Glue them onto the larger shield template.
4. Colour the small holder. Glue Fold twice where the diagonal lines meet the empty space.
5. Add glue to the back of the diagonal lines. Glue it vertically to the back of the shield

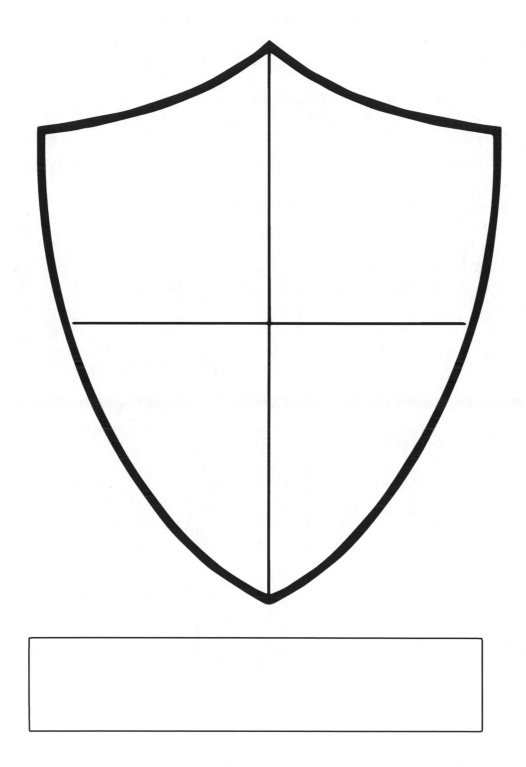

Breastplate Of Righteousness

A soldier used to wear a breastplate made of bronze or chain mail. It was fitted with loops or buckles that attached it to a thick belt, and covered the vital organs, like the heart. When we make decisions we need to listen to our hearts and feel for what is right.

1. Print and cut out the templates. You will need two of each.
2. Glue the pieces of the breastplate together onto butcher's paper.
3. Cut it out.
4. Cut out the scale template and trace (it may be better to have lots of scales premade) onto fancy paper.
5. Starting from the bottom, glue scales onto the assembled breastplate,
6. Cut out the neck strap pieces and then glue each piece onto a sheet of thin cardboard for strength.
7. Assemble the neck strap by gluing the circle to the front of the breastplate and the thinner strip to the back part, cutting each piece to the desired length.

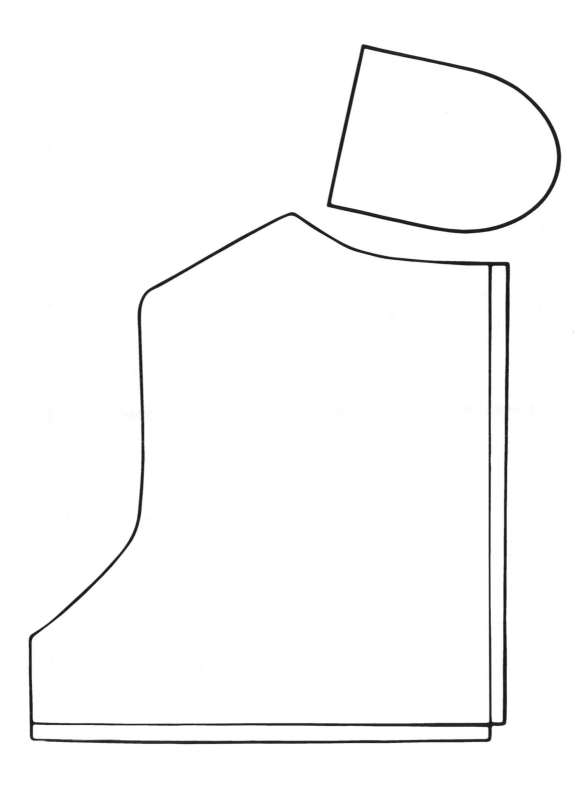

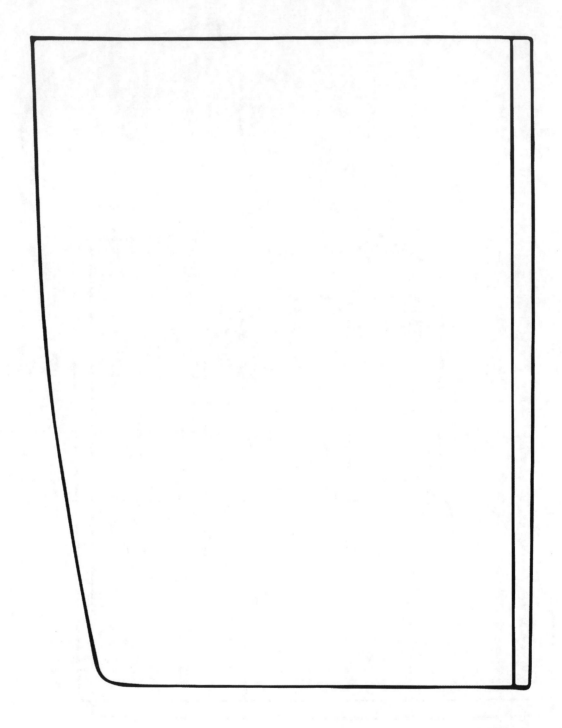

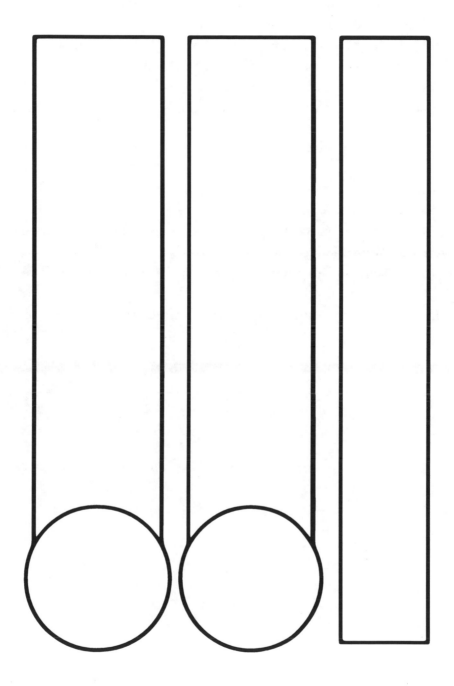

Belt Of Truth

Once upon a time almost everyone wore some sort of long sheet or light robe: like what you'd see in some Middle Eastern countries today. But, if you were a solider, this would cause a bit of a problem. A long robe would make it very difficult to move quickly and you would trip over your robe. It could also make you easier to grab. So the soldiers would take a belt to fasten all the extra fabric more tightly to their body. The belt of a Roman soldier was not a simple skinny leather strap like we wear today. It was a thick, heavy leather and metal band with a protective piece hanging down from the front of it. The belt held the soldier's sword and other weapons.

1. Cut out a long strip of black/brown paper, or glue two strips of black/brown to go around the child's waist.
2. You will need five copies of the long strip, preferably in black, and glue from the centre moving out towards the edges.
3. Print out the squares onto red paper and glue a small yellow circle to the middle of each red squares. (You will need 25 of each.)
4. Glue the red squares with yellow circles onto the long strips: you will need 5 squares on each.
5. To finish assembling the strips, use stickers, glitter or ornamentation to decorate the ends of each strip.

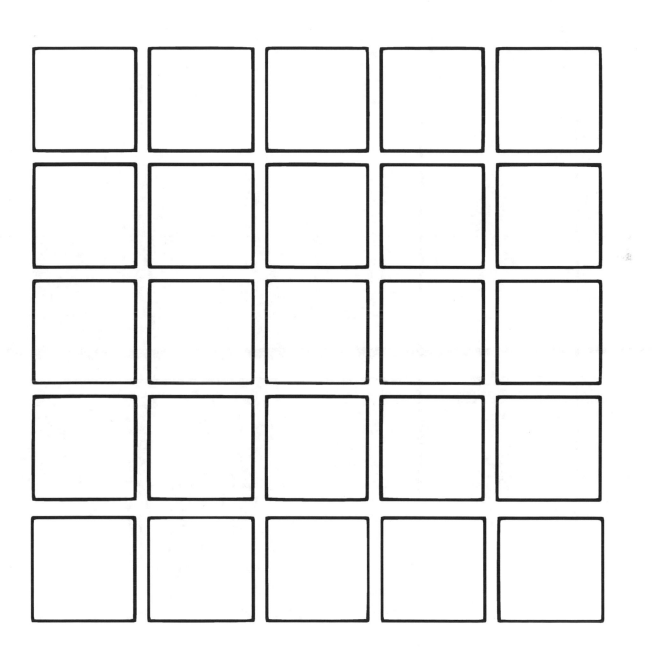

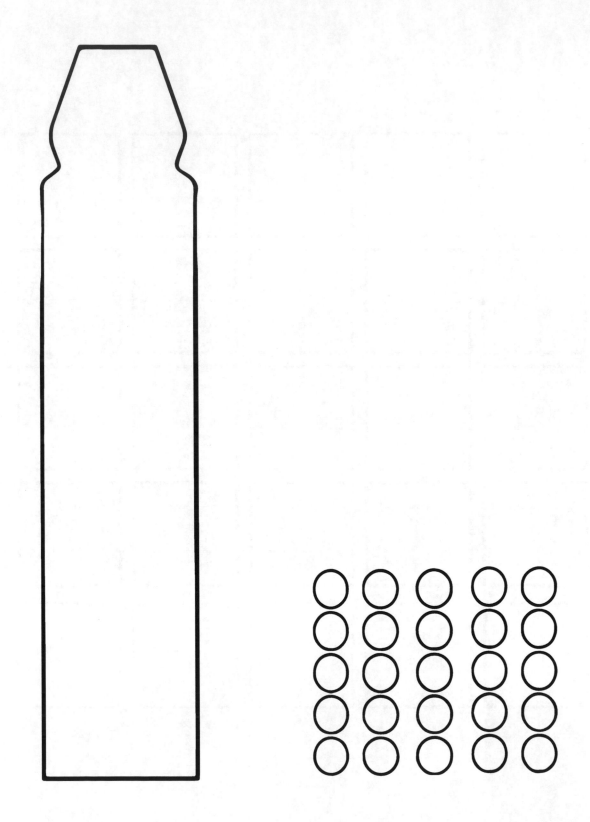

Sandals Of Peace

A victorious soldier had to be prepared for battle. They needed to have studied their enemy's plans and all the possible ways they might attack, be confident in their own plan of action, and have their feet firmly planted so that they could hold their ground when the attacks came.

1. Make sure the children have their shoes on
2. Trace around their foot onto thin cardboard (I stuck two pieces together), and cut out.
3. Using a hole punch, punch four holes into sandals
4. Take a metre long ribbon about 2cm wide and pock through the holes. wrap the ribbon in front of the leg and then back around the leg making a criss-cross pattern.
5. After criss-crossing a few times, tie the ribbon in the back to hold it up. Cut of any excess ribbon.

ABC through the Bible

This is a series of lessons that work off the principle that the stories and journeys of people through the Scriptures can speak to us today. Our purpose is to show and offer children a way of being. These lessons therefore focus on different emotions, and the way people react to them, in order to prepare children for real world experiences and encounters.

Books are in alphabetical order and a story or person from each letter has been picked out.

There are a few letters missing as they are not used for Bible books: f, q, u, v, x, y.

In life we go through a range of feelings and emotions. As we try to work out a way to deal with, process, and respond to our reactions to our feelings and emotions, we sometimes turn to other places, people and resources for help and inspiration.

One place we turn to as Christians is the Bible. The Bible is a collection of books, stories, letters, poems and songs, and over the next term or so, we will use these books to talk about some of the ways we feel and how to respond. *(Repeat this statement each week)*

Not every book of the Bible has a letter to go with it. So, over the coming weeks lets see who can pick the missing letters. As this is our first week, what letter will we be starting with...

A. Acts of the Apostles

Acts 9:1-31

Today we're working with the letter **A**.

And so, I wonder if anyone has ever been afraid of something.

I wonder what that could be? (Give own eg and acknowledge there answers)

Well, in the book the *Acts of the Apostles* there were some people who were afraid. Let's have a listen to what happened...

There was once a man named Saul who went about saying nasty things and threatening the friends of Jesus.

He went to the high priest and asked him for letters to the synagogues at Damascus, so that if he found any there who said they were friends of Jesus he might bring them bound to Jerusalem. But, when Saul was near Damascus, a light from heaven shone around him. He fell to the ground, and heard a voice saying to him, "Saul, Saul, why are you persecuting me?" And he said, "Who are you, Lord?" And he said, "I am Jesus, whom you are mistreating."

Saul rose from the ground, and although his eyes were opened, he couldn't see any more. So the people with him led Saul by the hand and brought him into Damascus.

Now there was a friend of Jesus at Damascus named Ananias. The Lord said to him in a vision, "Ananias go to Saul, and help him so that he might regain his sight." But Ananias answered, "Lord, I have heard from many about this man, how much evil he has done to your friends at Jerusalem." But the Lord said to him, "Go, for I will show him how he must live." So Ananias went and helped Saul and Saul immediately could see again.

For some days he was with the friends of Jesus at Damascus, but then he returned to Jerusalem. When he had come to Jerusalem, he attempted to join the friends of Jesus there. And they were all afraid of him, for they did not believe that he was a friendly person but someone who was going to be mean and nasty to them. But one of the group named Barnabas took him and brought him to them and declared to them how on the road he had seen the Lord, who spoke to him, and how at Damascus he had been kind and had changed and wasn't mean, cruel and nasty anymore. So Saul got to spend time with the friends of Jesus and join in with them.

So the church throughout all Judea and Galilee and Samaria had peace and was being built up.

Craft Activity: Wolf Mask (based on the old saying: who's afraid of the Big Bad Wolf). Print mask to size and cut out. Cloour and cut out. Cut out eyes and punch holes for string.

B. Book of Baruch

Baruch 2:21-26, 30, 34. 4:36-37

Today we're working with the letter **B**.

Belonging is central in our lives; it is so central that our words can never fully get to grips with the utter necessity of belonging. We feel Belonging in all sorts of ways: to a place, a person, a role, a relationship, an accomplishment, an ar, a duty, a community, God. Belonging is necessary for our freedom. To be at home somewhere (with a place, a person, a role, it doesn't matter, as long as it's somewhere) enables us to journey (to other places, other people, other roles, other relationships, other accomplishments, other encounters with God).

I wonder which places you belong to?

I wonder what that's like?

Well, in the book the *Book of Baruch* there were some people who were taken from the place they belonged to. Let's have a listen to what happened...

The Lord said: Bend your necks and serve the king of Babylon, and you will remain in the country that I gave to your family a long time ago. But if you do not listen to the voice of the Lord and serve the king of Babylon then everyone will be taken out of the towns of Judah and the streets of Jerusalem, and the whole country will be reduced to desert, with no inhabitants.'

But the people did not listen to the voice of the Lord and serve the king of Babylon, and so the Lord carried out what had been threatened and so, because of the naughtiness of the people of Israel and the people of Judah, you have made this place, that bears your name, what it is today.

But the Lord knew that, being stubborn people, they would not listen to him. But in the country of their exile, where all the people were taken, they will come to themselves. Then the Lord shall bring them back to their country and land that had been given to their ancestors Abraham, Isaac and Jacob, and make them masters in it again and they shall be home.

Jerusalem, turn your eyes to the east, see the joy that is coming to you from God. Look, the children you watched go away are on their way home; reassembled from east and west, the places where all the people were taken too, they are on their way home, rejoicing in God's glory.

Craft Activity: I belong with... Match the baby animal with its parent. They will need to cut and paste the baby animal to the back of the parent. Staple at side to form booklet.

C. 2 Chronicles

2 Chronicles 2:1-8

Today we're working with the letter *C*.

I wonder if any of you can tell me what cooperation means? *(Remember to work with their answers: cooperation is essentially the action or process of working together to the same end)*

Sometimes when we want to get something done we need people to help. Sometimes the thing we are trying to do is so big or difficult it needs lots of people to help out. Sometimes, that means some people do tiny simple tasks and others might be doing more complicated tasks at the same time. Big, or small, simple or difficult, each person's contribution to life and a community is needed for it to work.

In the book the *Book of Chronicles* there was a king who wanted to build an important buildings. Even though he was big and powerful do you think he could build it all by himself? I wonder what sort of people he needed to help him? Let's have a listen to what happened...

Solomon wanted to build a temple for God and a royal house for his kingship. Solomon picked seventy thousand men to carry materials, eighty thousand men to cut stone in the hills, and three thousand six hundred supervisors to watch over them to make sure they were ok and doing their jobs properly.

Solomon also sent a letter to Hiram the king of Tyre saying,

"As you did for David my father and sent him cedar trees in order to build for himself a house in which to dwell, *so deal with me*. I am going to build a temple for my God, sanctified for Him, for making sacrifices before Him, and for incense of fragrant spices, and for the continual showbread, for burnt offerings on both morning and evening, and for Sabbaths, New Moons, and appointed feasts of the Lord our God, as an ordinance forever for Israel. The house that I am building will be great because our God is greater than all other gods. Now may you send to me a wise man who works with gold, silver, bronze, iron, and in purple, crimson, and violet threads and knows how to engrave, who will be with the skilled workers and me in Judah and Jerusalem, which David my father established. And may you send me trees of cedar, cypress, and algum from Lebanon because I realize that your people know how to cut timber in Lebanon; and my people will be alongside your people, to prepare an abundance of timber for me, because the temple that I will build will be great and marvelous. I will provide crushed wheat, barley, wine, and oil for your workers who cut the timber."

There were lots of different people who needed to cooperate. I wonder which ones you can remember?

Craft Activity: Co operative Caterpillar

Making a cooperative caterpillar is not an individual craft. This will require everyone to take part in some way so when divvying up tasks, make sure each person is included.

You will need One person per colour to cut paper into strips.

Another person will then hand each person a strip of each colour, and depending on numbers, some glue.

Have another person draw on the eyes and mouth.

Have someone else roll thin strips of paper around a pencil to make antennae.

D. Daniel

Bel and the Dragon

Today we're working with the letter **D**.

I wonder if any of you can tell me what denial means? *(Remember to work with their answers: denial is a statement or action that rejects or refuses something.)*

Sometimes people say and do mean things when we can't see or hear them. Sometimes another person will come and tell us about this and we don't always believe them; we refuse to accept that what they tell us has happened. We deny it. It is always important to take time, sit back and think carefully through what we are told and check the facts so that we can find the truth.

In the book of *Daniel* there was a king who, when he was told the truth did not want to believe it until he saw evidence to show he was being tricked. Let's have a listen to what happened...

Once upon a time there was a king of Persia named Cyrus. His people had a statue they called Bel, and every day they gave it lots of flour, sheep and wine because the priests said it was a god. Even the king admired it and went every day to worship it. But Daniel, who was a friend of the king, worshiped his own God.

And the king said to him, "Why do you not worship Bel?" Daniel answered, "Because I do not worship statues, but the living God, who created everything."

The king said to him, "Do you not think that Bel is a living God? Do you not see how much he eats and drinks every day?"

Then Daniel laughed, and said, "Do not be tricked, king Cyrus; for this is only clay inside and brass outside, and it never ate or drank anything."

Then the king was angry, and he called the priests and said to them, "If you do not tell me who is eating the food we give, you shall die. But if you prove that Bel is eating them, Daniel shall die, because he said these things." Daniel replied; "that's fine as I know I am telling the truth."

And the priests of Bel said; "We will go outside, and you king, put the flour, sheep and wine inside and shut the door and seal it with your signet. And when you return in the morning, if you do not find that Bel has eaten it all, we will die; or else Daniel will, as he is telling lies about us."

When the priests had left, the king put out the food for Bel. Then Daniel ordered his servants to bring ashes and they spread them across the whole floor with only the king seeing them do this. Then they went out, shut the door and sealed it with the king's signet, and departed. The priests were not worried, because beneath the table they had made a hidden entrance, and this is how they would take the things. In the night the priests and their families came and ate and drank everything.

Early in the morning the king and Daniel went to the room with the statue in it. And the king asked; "Are the seals on the door broken, Daniel?" Daniel answered, "They are unbroken."

The king opened the door and as soon as the doors were opened, the king looked at the table, and seeing the food had all gone, shouted in a loud voice, "You are great, O Bel; and with you there is no deceit, none at all."

Then Daniel laughed, and restrained the king from going in, and said, "Look at the floor, and notice whose footsteps these are." The king said, "I see the footsteps of people."

Then the king was enraged, and he seized the priests and they showed him the secret doors. There was also a great dragon they worshipped as well. And the king said to Daniel, "You cannot deny that this is a living god; so why not worship him?"

Daniel said, "I will worship my God, for he is the living God. But if you, O king, will give me permission, I will slay the dragon without sword or club." The king said, "I give you permission."

Then Daniel took pitch, fat, and hair, and boiled them together and made cakes, which he fed to the dragon. The dragon ate them, and burst open. And Daniel said, "See what you have been worshiping! It was a trick by those naughty priests as well."

Craft Activity: A dancing Dragon. This is a paper dragon based on dragon totem flags I saw in China

1. *Copy dragon onto cardboard. It is a double-sided dragon so each person needs one copy.*
2. *Colour in using textas or crayons.*
3. *Cut out pieces. Fold head in half and cut out the space in the mouth.*
4. *Cut a red A4 piece of paper into thirds length ways. One of these will be the body of each dragon.*
5. *Using the concertina fold, fold the body.*
6. *Glue the head to one end and the tail to each end of the body, sticking a paddle pop stick into the head fold.*
7. *Glue legs just behind the head.*
8. *Rip some yellow tissue paper and add to the mouth.*

E. Esther

The Book of Esther

Today we're working with the letter *E*.

I wonder if any of you can tell me what empathy means? *(Remember to work with their answers: it is the ability to sense other people's emotions, coupled with the ability to imagine what someone else might be thinking or feeling.)*

Sometimes bad things and it makes people sad. Empathy creates connections between people, bringing us together and helping to forge friendships and love. It makes us feel as if someone cares for us: without it we would likely feel vulnerable and lonely. When we connect and care about each other, the world becomes a nicer place to live.

In the book of *Esther* there was a woman who had empathy.

Let's have a listen to what happened...

Three years after Xerxes became the King of Persia (he was the grandson of King Cyrus from our last story), he celebrated by throwing a long party for everyone that went for 180 days. After this Xerxes hosted a smaller week-long party for the people of the capital city of Shushan. On the last day of this party he commanded his wife Vashti to the party so that he could show them how beautiful she was. Vashti said no! Vashti was executed.

But then Xerxes was lonely. His servants suggested that he orchestrate a beauty pageant. Officers would be appointed in all the king's lands, and all beautiful girls would be brought to Xerxes. And the girl he picked would be the new queen.

The leader of the Jews was named Mordechai. He had a cousin, Esther, who was orphaned as a young girl. Mordechai raised her and treated her as a daughter. Though she had no desire to be the queen, Esther was forcibly taken to the king's harem, to participate in the contest. While all the other contestant beautified themselves with perfumes and lotions, Esther did nothing. When Esther appeared before the king, he immediately liked her, and Esther became the new Queen of Persia. But as per Mordechai's directive, Esther refused to tell anyone her nationality—even to the king.

Shortly after Esther became queen, Mordechai overheard two of the king's chamberlains discussing a plot to assassinate the king. Mordechai had them reported, and the traitors were hanged. Meanwhile, Haman, one of Xerxes' ministers, was promoted to the position of Prime Minister. Haman was a Jew hater. Immediately after his promotion, the king issued a decree ordering everyone to bow down whenever Haman appeared. Now Haman would walk around with a large idol hanging from a chain around his neck. When Mordechai, a proud Jew, refused to bow down, Haman was infuriated. He resolved to take revenge against all the Jews and threw lots to determine the "lucky" day when he would implement his plan. Haman approached Xerxes and offered him 10,000 silver talents in exchange for permission to exterminate the Jews. Xerxes, who was no friend of the Jews either, said 'yes'. Haman immediately sent proclamations to all the king's land. These declarations, sealed with the royal signet ring, ordered the people to rise up against the Jews and kill them all on the set date.

Mordechai became aware of the decree and was very upset. He sent a message to Esther, asking her to approach the king and beg him to spare her people. Esther responded that according to the rules anyone who entered the king's presence un-summoned would be put to death—unless the king extended to that person his golden scepter. "And I," Esther said, "have not been summoned by the king for thirty days already!"

Mordechai sent another message: "Do not think that you will escape the fate of all the Jews by being in the king's palace. For if you will remain silent at this time, relief and salvation will come to the Jews from another source, and you and the house of your father will be lost. And who knows if it is not for just such a time that you reached this royal position."

Esther agreed to approach the king. But she asked Mordechai to gather all the Jews and let them all fast for three days and nights. And after this fast Esther would put her life in her hands and approach the king. Mordechai complied with Esther's request. He gathered the Jews – especially the children, 22,000 of them – and they fasted, repented and prayed to G-d.

After three days of fasting, Esther donned royal garb and entered Xerxes' chambers. Immediately, the king extended his scepter. "What is it?" Xerxes asked. "What is your request?"

"I would like to invite the king and Haman to a small feast I have prepared," Esther responded.

So the king and Haman joined Esther for a wine-feast. During the feast, the king again asked Esther whether she had anything to request. "Yes," Esther responded. "I would appreciate if tomorrow, again, the king and Haman would join me for a feast. And then I will tell the king my request. Haman left the party a happy and proud man. But standing at the king's gate was Mordechai – who *still* refused to bow to Haman – and Haman was enraged. When he arrived home, his wife and wise advisors counseled him to erect a gallows, and then to go to the king and request permission to hang Mordechai. Haman excitedly went ahead and put up the gallows.

Sleep eluded the king that night, so he asked his servants to read for him from the Royal Chronicles. They complied with the king's orders. They read from the Chronicles how Mordechai saved the king's life when two of his chamberlains hatched a plot to kill him. "Was he rewarded for this fine act?" Xerxes asked. "No he was not," the servants responded.

At that moment Haman entered the king's courtyard. His purpose? To ask the king's permission to hang Mordechai! Before Haman could utter a word, Xerxes addressed him: "My Haman, in your estimation, what shall be done to a person whom the king wishes to honour?"

Haman, who was certain that the king wished to honour him, responded: "Bring royal garment and a royal horse. And let one of the king's nobles dress the man and lead him on the horse through the city streets, proclaiming before him, 'So is done for the man whom the king wishes to honour!'"

"Great idea," Xerxes responded. "Now go get the garments and the horse and do so for Mordechai the Jew!" Haman had no choice but to comply. On the next day he went and honoured Mordechai as the king had ordered, and then immediately rushed to join the king and Esther for the Second Feast.

"What is your request?" a curious King Xerxes asked Esther at the feast.

"If I have found favour in your eyes, O King," Esther pleaded, "and if it pleases the king, let my life be granted me by my plea, and the life of my people by my request. For my people and I have been sold to be annihilated, killed and destroyed!" Esther then identified Haman as the evil person who wished to perpetrate this atrocity. The king was greatly angered. When he was then informed that Haman had built a gallows for Mordechai, he ordered that Haman be hanged on that very gallows.

The lovely Queen Esther who risks her own life to defend her people, is the one with whom we empathize, the model we would emulate, the person who impels us to be courageous, to stand up for bullied people and risk all for the kingdom.

Craft Activity: Listening Ears. Colour and cut out. Make a headband with two strips of paper and stick ears on. Stick the My Listening Ears! Onto the front of headband.

My Listening Ears!

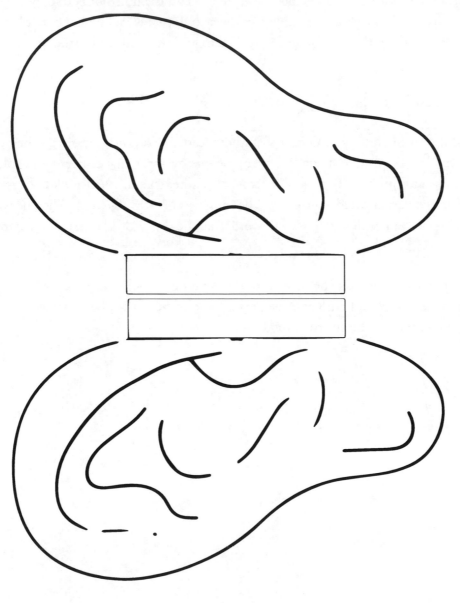

180

G. Genesis

Genesis 49:1-50:14

Today we're working with the letter **G**.

I wonder if any of you can tell me what grief means? *(Remember to work with their answers: it is a natural response to losing someone or something that's important to you. You may feel a variety of emotions, like sadness or loneliness. And you might experience it for a number of different reasons. Maybe a loved one died, a relationship ended, or you lost your job).*

At some point we all feel grief. It is normal and can take time to process, to work with.

In the book of *Genesis* there is a story of a man named Jacob who died.

Let's have a listen to what happened...

Jacob had lived a very long life. He called his family to come to him and said to them, "I am about to be gathered to my people. Bury me with my fathers in the cave that is in the field of Ephron the Hittite, in the cave that is in the field of Machpelah, which is before Mamre in the land of Canaan, which Abraham bought along with the field from Ephron the Hittite as a burial place. They buried Abraham and Sarah his wife there. They buried Isaac and Rebekah his wife there, and I buried Leah there. The field and the cave that is there were purchased from the children of Heth."

When Jacob finished instructing his sons, he drew his feet into the bed, breathed his last, and was gathered to his people. Then Joseph fell on his father's face and wept over him and kissed him. Joseph commanded his servants the physicians to embalm his father. So the physicians embalmed Israel. Forty days were required for him, for such is the time required for those who are embalmed. Then the Egyptians mourned for him seventy days.

When the days of his mourning were past, Joseph spoke to the household of Pharaoh, saying, "If now I have found favor in your eyes, speak to Pharaoh, saying, My father made me swear, saying, "I am about to die. Bury me in my tomb which I dug for myself in the land of Canaan." Now therefore please let me go up and bury my father, and then I will return.' " Pharaoh said, "Go up and bury your father, as he made you swear to do."

Joseph went up to bury his father, and all the servants of Pharaoh went up with him too, the elders of his household and all the elders of the land of Egypt, all the house of Joseph and his brothers and his father's household. They left only their little ones and their flocks and their herds in the land of Goshen. Both the chariots and horsemen also went up with him. It was a very great company.

When they came to the threshing floor of Atad, which is beyond the Jordan, they mourned with a great and very sorrowful lamentation. He observed seven days of mourning for his father. When the inhabitants of the land, the Canaanites, saw the mourning at the threshing floor of Atad, they said, "This is a grievous mourning for the Egyptians."

Craft Activity: Embraced in love we cannot always see.

Print and cut out the heart. Using the heart as a template get children to cut a heart out of red, pink or blue cardboard.

Trace children's hands onto a sheet of white or decorative cardboard. They'll love helping with this part! Cut out the hands. Attach the hands at either end of a ribbon

Tape the middle of the string to the back of the big heart

H. Habakkuk

Habakkuk 2:2-19

Today we're working with the letter **H**.

I wonder if any of you can tell me what heavy-hearted means? *(Remember to work with their answers: it is a sense of Melancholy; of being depressed; or sad. When your heart is weighted down by sorrow).*

At some point we all feel a bit this way. We all will feel heavy-hearted. So will other people. When we see people feeling heavy-hearted, we can always be there to show them some love and offer help and reassurance.

In the book of *Habbakkak* there is a story of a man who was heavy-hearted because the people had started to build the temple but work had stopped as they didn't want to keep paying for it or give their time to finish the job.

Let's have a listen to what happened...

I was very sad and heavy-hearted. We had hoped to build the new temple but it wasn't getting built. We were all having a hard time. I cried to God and God answered me saying: Write this down; Make it plain upon tablets, so that the one who read it may run. For the vision is a witness for the appointed time, a testimony to the end; it will not disappoint. If it delays, wait for it, it will surely come, it will not be late. See, the rash have no integrity; but the just one who is righteous because of faith shall live. Indeed wealth is treacherous; a proud person does not succeed. Those who open wide their throats like Sheol, and is insatiable as death, Who gathers to themself all the nations, and collects for themself all the peoples— Shall not all these take up a taunt against them, and make a riddle, saying:

Ah! you who store up what is not yours
—how long can it last!—
you who load yourself down with collateral.
Will your debtors* not rise suddenly?
Will they not awake, those who make you tremble?
You will become their spoil!
Because you plundered many nations,
the remaining peoples shall plunder you;
Because of the shedding of human blood,
and violence done to the land,
to the city and to all who live in it.

Ah! you who pursue evil gain for your household,
setting your nest on high
to escape the reach of misfortune!
You have devised shame for your household,
cutting off many peoples, forfeiting your own life;
For the stone in the wall shall cry out,[*]
and the beam in the frame shall answer it!
Ah! you who build a city by bloodshed,
and who establish a town with injustice!

Just wait and hope for the earth shall be filled with the knowledge of the God's glory, and how much you are loved: just as the water covers the sea.

When we see people feeling heavy-hearted, we can always be there to show them some love and offer help and reassurance.

I wonder when you may have felt like this?

I wonder what things you can do to help others feel a bit better?

I wonder how we can help people feel light-hearted?

Craft Activity: the gift of growing love. Copy and colour the stems in. Paint the children's hand and get them to 'stamp' it onto a blank piece of paper (painting their hands enables the paint to be thin and dry quickly). Cut around handprint and stick onto the stem as flowers.

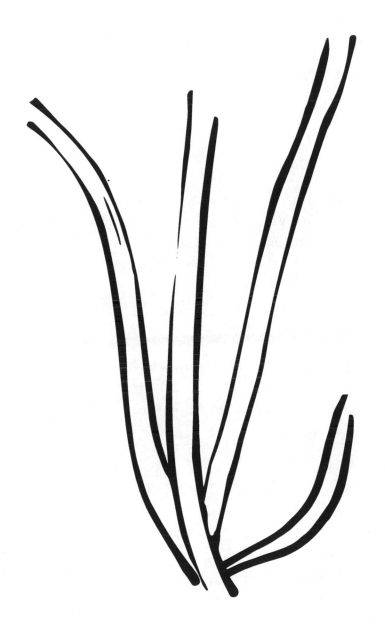

I. Isaiah

Isaiah 6:1-50:14

Today we're working with the letter *I*.

I wonder if any of you can tell me what feeling inadequate means? *(Remember to work with their answers: it is a sense that one lacks the quality or quantity required; that they are insufficient for a purpose.).*

In the book of *Isaiah* there is a story of a man who felt inadequate and wasn't good enough to be near God.

Let's have a listen to what happened...

In the year that King Uzziah died, Isaiah saw a dream of God as King of the Universe sitting on a throne, high and lifted up, and the train of God's robe filled the entire temple. Above the throne stood a type of angel called seraphim; each one had six wings: with two he covered his face, with two he covered his feet, and two he used to fly. And one cried to another and said:
"Holy, holy, holy is the Lord of hosts;
The whole earth is full of His glory!"
At the sound of their voice the posts of the door were shaken, and the house was filled with smoke.
Isaiah said:
"Woe is me, for I am undone and about to be destroyed!
Because I am a man of unclean lips,
And I dwell in the midst of a people of unclean lips;
For my eyes have seen the King,
The Lord of hosts."

Then one of the seraphim went and, using tongs, took a live coal from the altar and flew to Isaiah, and he touched Isaiah's mouth with it, and said:
"Behold, this has touched your lips;
Your iniquity is taken away,
And all that makes you feel inadequate has been taken away. You are able to be all you aim to be."

Craft Activity: paper doll. Like us, this girl can grow to become whatever she chooses to be, or to do whatever she strives to do.

I Can Be All I Want to Be

I Am Adequate

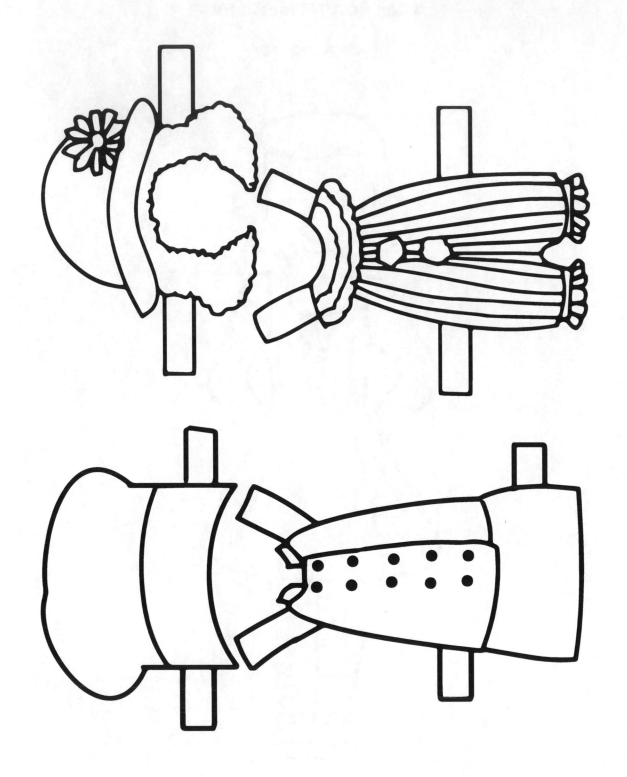

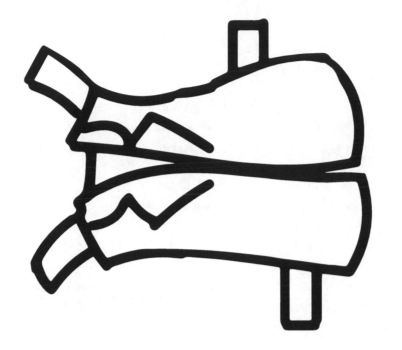

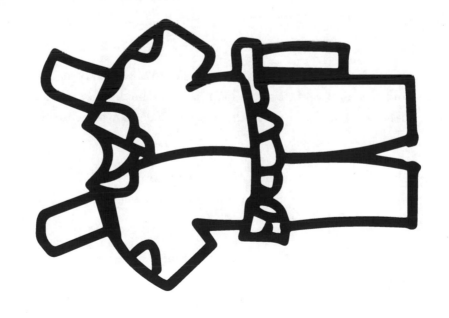

J. Judith

The Book of Judith

Today we're working with the letter *J*.

I wonder if any of you can tell me what feeling judgmental means? *(Remember to work with their answers: it is a sense concerning the use of judgement; 'judgemental decisions about the likelihood of company survival'. Having or displaying an overly critical point of view; 'I don't like to sound judgemental, but it was a big mistake'.*

In the book of *Judith* there is a story of a widow who judges Israel in the time of military crisis.

Let's have a listen to what happened...

Once upon a time there was a king named Nebuchadnezzar, who ruled over the Assyrians in the great city of Nineveh. When he had been king for 12 years he decided to go to war against king Arphaxad who was ruling over the Medes in Ecbatana.

King Nebuchadnezzar contacted all the inhabitants of the lands, both near and far to join his war but all the inhabitants of the whole land made light of the summons of Nebuchadnezzar, and would not join him in the war. They were not afraid of him, since he was only a single opponent. So they sent back his envoys empty-handed and disgraced. Then Nebuchadnezzar fell into a violent rage against all the land, and swore by his throne and his kingdom that he would take revenge on all the lands.

Seven yeas later King Nebuchadnezzar won and began to take his revenge. He summoned all his attendants and officers, and told them his plan. King Nebuchadnezzar summoned Holofernes, the general of his forces, and sent him on the mission to destroy all who had refused to obey the order he had issued.

Then he and all his forces set out on their expedition ito overrun all the lands with their chariots, cavalry, and picked infantry. Fear and dread of Holofernes fell upon all the inhabitants of the land. Soon many began to surrender.

When the Israelites who lived in Judea heard of all that Holofernes had done to the nations, and utterly destroyed them, they were in very great fear of him, and greatly alarmed for Jerusalem and the temple of their God. They secured all the high hilltops, fortified the villages on them, and since their fields had recently been harvested, stored up provisions in preparation for war.

Joakim, who was high priest in Jerusalem wrote to the other lands and instructed them to keep firm hold of the mountain passes, since these offered access to Judea. It would be easy to stop those advancing, as the approach was only wide enough for two at a time.

The Israelites carried out the orders. And as they prepared for war, the Israelites cried out to God. God heard their cry and saw their distress. The people continued fasting for many days throughout Judea and before the sanctuary of the Lord Almighty in Jerusalem.

It was reported to Holofernes that the Israelites were ready for battle, had blocked the mountain passes, fortified the high hilltops, and placed roadblocks in the plains.

"We are not afraid of the Israelites," they said, "for they are a powerless people, incapable of a strong defense. Therefore let us attack, master Holofernes. They will become fodder for your great army." So off they went to attack. They surrounded the Israelites and cut off their water supply. The Israelites cried out and were beginning to plan to surrender. The widow Judith heard of this.

She was beautiful in appearance and very lovely to behold. Her husband, Manasseh, had left her gold and silver, male and female servants, livestock and fields, which she was maintaining. No one had a bad word to say about her, for she feared God greatly.

So when Judith heard of the harsh words of the people, discouraged by their lack of water, she sent her maid who was in charge of all her things to summon the leaders of her city.

When they came, she said to them: "Listen to me, you rulers of the people. What you said to the people today is not right. You promised to hand over the city to our enemies unless within a certain time the Lord comes to our aid. Who are you to put God to the test today, setting yourselves in the place of God in human affairs? You will never understand anything!". Judith came up with a plan and set out to put it in motion. She washed her body with water, and anointed herself with rich ointment. She arranged her hair, put on a diadem, and dressed in the festive attire. She chose sandals for her feet, and put on her anklets, bracelets, rings, earrings, and all her other jewelry. She gave her maid a skin of wine and a jug of oil. She filled a bag with roasted grain, dried fig cakes, and pure bread. She wrapped all her dishes and gave them to the maid to carry and left to go to the enemy's army. She told their soldiers she was trying to run away and had come to tell Holofernes the best way to attack without any of his soldiers being killed. They took her to him and he found her so beautiful that he invited her to eat with him. Judith said she had to use her own things because it would be a scandal if she did. When they were alone they began to drink. He drank a lot of wine and she only pretended and when he fell asleep took his sword, chopped of his head, put it in a bag and ran back to the Israelites city. There she ordered them to get ready for battle and attack. The enemy were in such a disarray without their leader they were easily defeated and ran away

Craft Activity: Lion mask. People judge all the time: sometimes rightly and sometimes unfairly. We must always have the strength and pride of a lion and do everything in such a way that if we can do it we do it, and if we can't, we find a way to do it right.

K. Kings

1 kings 3:16-28

Today we're working with the letter ***K***.

I wonder if any of you can tell me what knowledgeable means? *(Remember to work with their answers: it is a sense of having or demonstrating knowledge, insight, or understanding. It also means being intelligent; well informed; discerning; perceptive'.*

In the book of *Kings* there is a story of a King who needed to be knowledgeable in order to govern wisely.

Let's have a listen to what happened...

Once upon a time there were two women came to the king and stood before him. One of the women said, "Oh, my lord, this woman and I live in the same house, and I gave birth to a child while she was in the house. Then, three days later after this woman also gave birth to a baby. We were alone. There was no one else with us in the house. Sadly, during the night this woman's son died because she lay on him. She then got up at midnight and took my son from beside me, while I slept, and laid him at her breast, and laid her dead son at my breast. When I woke in the morning to nurse my child, behold, he was dead. But when I looked at him closely it was clear he was not the child that I had borne." But the other woman said, "No, the living child is mine, and the dead child is yours." The first said, "No, the dead child is yours, and the living child is mine." And they argued like this in front of the king.

Then the king came up with a way to work out who was the real mother, and said, "One of you says this is my son that is alive, and your son is dead and the other that your son is dead, and my son is the living one. So bring me a sword and I will sort this out." So a sword was brought before the king. And the king said, "Divide the living child in two, and give half to the one and half to the other." Then the woman whose son was alive said to the king, because her heart yearned for her son, "Oh, my King, give her the living child, and by no means put him to death." But the other said, "He shall be neither mine nor yours; cut him in half." Then the king answered and said, "Give the living child to the first woman, and by no means put him to death; she is his mother."

When everyone heard of the judgment that the king had made they stood in awe of him, because they perceived that he was wise in working out judgment.

Craft Activity: Secret Decoder. In life we start off knowing nothing. What we know we learn throughout out lives. When we don't know something, we need to find ways to access the information. Like a spy trying to decode a secret message, we need to have enough material and information to carefully think through and consider the evidence and material in front of us to make knowledgeable decisions.

To make: Stick wheels onto of each other, biggest to smallest. Pock hole through the centre and stick a split pin through the hole.

To use: Pick a letter on the bottom wheel (1) and a number on the middle circle (2). This then becomes your unique key. When they then are lined up, write your message using the letters on the centre wheel to represent the letters on the bottom wheel.

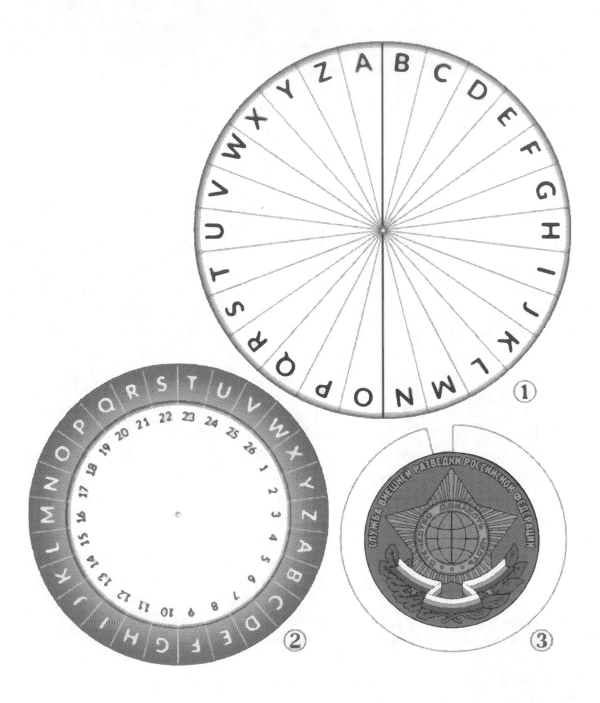

L. Luke

Luke 5:12-16

Today we're working with the letter **L**.

I wonder if any of you can tell me what loneliness means? *(Remember to work with their answers: Loneliness is a complex and usually unpleasant emotional response to isolation. Loneliness typically includes anxious feelings about a lack connection or communication with other beings, both in the present and extending into the future. As such, loneliness can be felt even when surrounded by other people.'.*

Everyone has lonely moments in life, but when loneliness begins to define our lives, it causes serious problems. We compromise our principles to try to fill the emotional emptiness. We choose behaviour that harms our health, relationships, and finances.

In the Gospel according to *Luke* Jesus would feel lonely even when with other people.

Let's have a listen to what happened...

Once when Jesus arrived in one of the towns, he was immediately recognized, and word spread like wildfire. A man came along who was covered with a terrible skin disease. He saw Jesus, fell facedown and begged Him, "Lord, if YOU are willing, YOU can make me clean."
Jesus reached out His hand and touched the man. "I am willing," He said, "be clean!" And immediately the terrible skin disease was cured.
"Do not tell anyone," Jesus instructed him. "But go, show yourself to the priest and present the offering Moses prescribed for your cleansing, as a testimony to them."
But the news about Jesus spread all the more, and great crowds came to hear Him and to be healed of their sicknesses. In all of this, the crowds though did not want Jesus. They wanted something from Jesus. And there was a deep, subtle loneliness to always being merely useful to (or used by) others. The utter lack of concern and the insatiable expectation of entitlement and even brazen disappointment with Jesus meant that Jesus frequently withdrew to the wilderness to pray.

Craft Activity: Tea Cup. In life we all will feel lonely. We need to make sure we still look after ourselves and, when the people we care about look lonely, that we are there for them as well. One way to do this is to play with them, or to visit, listen to them and even just have a cup of tea or coffee with them.

To make the mug, copy and colour the picture. Cut on all solid black lines (do not cut the handle in half). Fold all dotted lines. Slide handle tabs into slots on side of mug and stick down and hold in place for a minute. Stick all tabs into place.

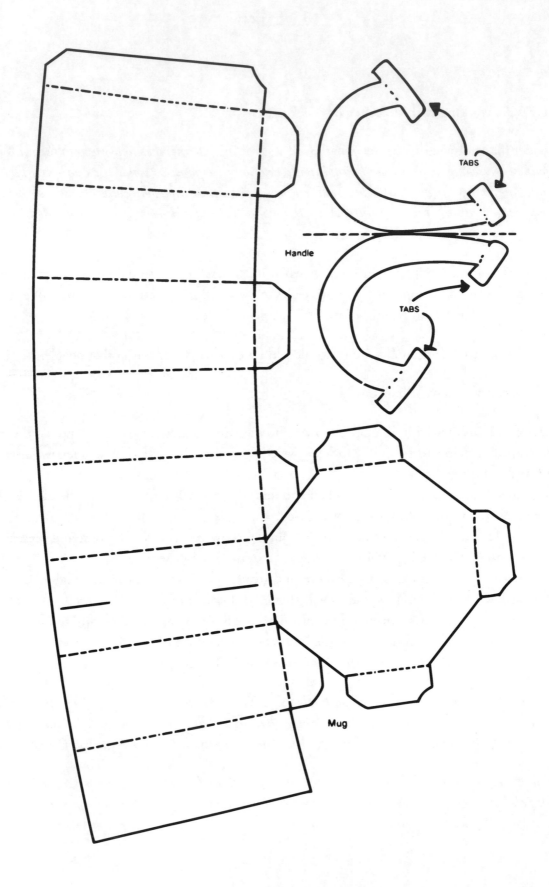

Handle

TABS

TABS

Mug

M. Maccabees

2 Maccabees 7:1-38

Today we're working with the letter *M*.

I wonder if any of you can tell me what motherly means? *(Remember to work with their answers: it is a resemblance, or characteristic of a mother, especially in being caring, protective, and kind'.*

Everyone can be motherly, because we can all be caring, nurturing, loving, devoted, affectionate, warm, tender, gentle, protective and kind.

In the 2nd book of *Maccabees* there is the story of a mother.

Let's have a listen to what happened...

Once an evil king sent an Athenian senator to force the Jews to abandon the laws of their ancestors and live no longer by the laws of God, but some stayed true to what their mother's had taught them. Most admirable and worthy of everlasting remembrance was the mother of seven boys who kept doing the right thing even though the evil king then had them killed. This mother watched as her seven sons perished in a single day. She bore it courageously because of her hope in the Lord. Filled with a noble spirit that stirred her, she exhorted each of them in the language of their ancestors with these words: "I do not know how you came to be in my womb; it was not I who gave you breath and life, nor was it I who arranged the elements you are made of. Therefore, since it is the Creator of the universe who shaped the beginning of humankind and brought about the origin of everything, he, in his mercy, will give you back both breath and life, because you now disregard yourselves for the sake of his law."

This example of a mother reminds us that no matter how hard we try to protect others and teach them the right thing, bad things can still happen. Accidents can still happen. And even then, when we have hurt ourselves those who are motherly to us are still there with us being loving, affectionate, and tender.

Craft Activity: Mother's Day card. A mother kangaroo carries and cares for her baby joey; looking after it and keeping it close and safe like our mothers try to do with us.

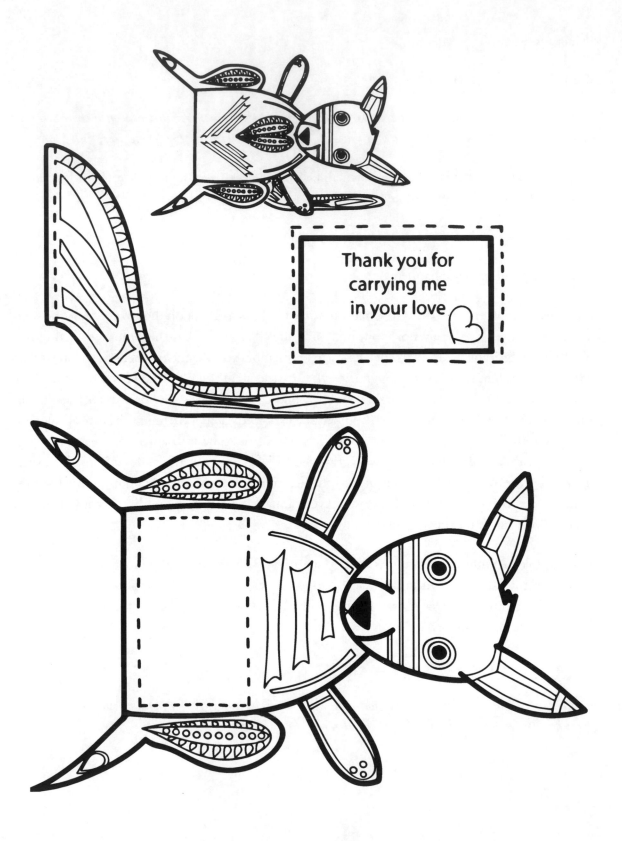

Thank you for
carrying me
in your love

198

N. Nehemiah

Nehemiah 1-3:38

Today we're working with the letter *N*.

I wonder if any of you can tell me what negative means? *(Remember to work with their answers: it is expressing a refusal or negation).*

We can be a bit negative, but that is not the same as being negative people. Negative people go around shutting down other people's ideas or dreams and because of this are not nice to be around. You need to make sure you do not listen to people laughing at your ideas and trying to put them down.

In the book of *Nehemiah* there is the story of people who were being negative.

Let's have a listen to what happened...

There was once a man named Nehemiah. One day his brother came with men from Judah and Nehemiah asked them concerning the Jews who escaped, who had survived the exile, and concerning Jerusalem. They said; "The remnant there in the province who had survived the exile is in great trouble and shame. The wall of Jerusalem is broken down, and its gates are destroyed by fire." When Nehemiah heard this he sat down and wept and mourned for days. Nehemiah went to the king and asked, "If it pleases the king, let letters be given me to the governors of the province Beyond the River, that they may let me pass through until I come to Judah, and a letter to Asaph, the keeper of the king's forest, that he may give me timber to make beams for the gates of the fortress of the temple, and for the wall of the city, and for the house that I shall occupy." And the king granted Nehemiah what he asked, for and he set off. During the night, Nehemiah went out by the Valley Gate to the Dragon Spring and to the Dung Gate, and inspected the walls of Jerusalem that were broken down and its gates that had been destroyed by fire. Then he went on to the Fountain Gate and to the King's Pool and then inspected the wall, Then Nehemiah said to those who were with him, "You see the trouble we are in, how Jerusalem lies in ruins with its gates burned. Come, let us build the wall of Jerusalem, that we may no longer suffer derision." They said, "Let us rise up and build." So they strengthened their hands for the good work. But when Sanballat the Horonite and Tobiah the Ammonite servant and Geshem the Arab heard of it, they jeered at and despised them and said, "What is this thing that you are doing? And when Sanballat heard they were rebuilding the wall, he became angry and very much incensed. He ridiculed the Jews, saying in the presence of his associates and the troops of Samaria: "What are these miserable Jews trying to do? Will they complete their restoration in a single day? Will they recover these stones, burnt as they are, from the heaps of dust?" Tobiah the Ammonite was beside him, and he said: "Whatever they are building—if a fox attacks it, it will breach their wall of stones!" In the end though, the wall was built.

Craft Activity: Negative Numbat paddle pop characters. Print out and colour. Stick to paddle pop sticks

O. Obadiah

Obadiah 1:1-21

Today we're working with the letter **O**.

I wonder if any of you can tell me what ominous means? *(Remember to work with their answers: it is the worrying impression that something bad is going to happen).*

Sometimes we know that things don't feel right. We have the feeling that something bad is about to happen. When we feel like this we shoul stop and think carefully, change what we are doing, and make sure we are somewhere safe.

In the book of *Obadiah* there is the story of someone who had the feeling something ominous was about to happen.

Let's have a listen to what happened...

There was once a man named Obadiah who felt something ominous was about to occur. Obadiah felt that the people were going to rise up and go to war against Edom because they were utterly contemptible. The pride of their heart Edom had deceived them, dwelling in their lofty homes, who say in their heart, "Who will bring me down to earth?"

Though they soar like the eagle, and their nest is set among the stars,

From there they will be brought down. To the border they will be driven. All their allies and partners have deceived them and have overpowered Edom;

Those who eat your bread will replace you with foreigners, who have no understanding.

On that day God will make the wise disappear from Edom, and understanding from Mount Esau? Teman, your warriors will be terror-stricken, so that everyone on Mount Esau will be cut down. Because of violence to your brother Jacob, disgrace will cover you, you will be done away with forever!

On the day you stood by, the day strangers carried off his possessions, And foreigners entered his gates and cast lots for Jerusalem, you too were like one of them. Do not gloat over the day of your brother, the day of his disaster;

Do not exult over the people of Judah on the day of their ruin; Do not speak haughtily on the day of distress!

Near is the day of the LORD against all the nations! As you have done, so will it be done to you, your conduct will come back upon your own head; As you drank upon my holy mountain, so will all the nations drink continually. Yes, they will drink and swallow, and will become as though they had not been. But on Mount Zion there will be some who escape the mountain will be holy, and the house of Jacob will take possession of those who dispossessed them. Deliverers will ascend Mount Zion to rule Mount Esau, and the kingship shall be God's.

Craft Activity: Storm Clouds. Print the clouds onto black, grey and white paper. Cut and stick to make a cloud formation. Stick cotton wool balls for extra effect. Add raindrops to complete the picture.

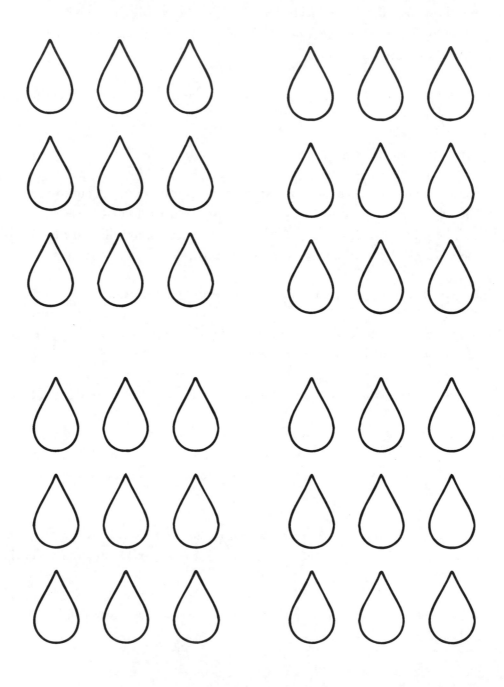

P. Peter

1 Peter 1:3-12

Today we're working with the letter **P**.

I wonder if any of you can tell me what positive means? *(Remember to work with their answers: it is being constructive, optimistic, or confident.)*.

Being positive is when we are looking towards the good side of things, showing certainty and exhibiting all our good – all our positive- emotions.

In the First Letter of *Peter* we are given an example of a positive outlook.

Let's have a listen to what happened...

Peter wrote: Blessed be the God and Father of our Lord Jesus Christ, who in his great mercy gave us a new birth into a living hope through the resurrection of Jesus Christ from the dead **in**to an inheritance that is imperishable, undefiled, unfading, and kept in heaven for you. By the power of God you are safeguarded through faith, to a salvation that is ready to be revealed in the final time. Even though you may now suffer through various trials for a little while still rejoice, so that the genuineness of your faith, (which is more precious than gold that is perishable even though tested by fire), may prove to be for praise, glory, and honour at the revelation of Jesus. For, although you have not seen him, you love him; even though you do not see him now yet believe in him, you rejoice with an indescribable and glorious joy, as you attain the goal of your faith, that is, the salvation of your souls.

When it comes to this salvation, prophets who prophesied about the grace that was to be yours searched and investigated it, nvestigating the time and circumstances that the Spirit of Christ within them indicated when it testified in advance to the sufferings destined for Christ and the glories to follow them. It was revealed to them that they were serving not themselves but you with regard to the things that have now been announced to you by those who preached the good news to you through the holy Spirit sent from heaven, things into which angels longed to look.

Craft Activity: Anger Catcher.

Step 1: Print out anger catcher. Colour the triangles. Cut out the anger catcher once coloured and place face down.

Step 2: Fold each corner towards the centre so that the numbers and colours are facing you.

Step 3: Turn it over and again fold each corner into the centre so that the colour names are visible.

Step 4: Fold it in half so that the colour names are touching and the numbers are on the outside. Now open it and fold it in half the other way.

Step 5: Insert your thumb and first finger of each hand (pinching motion) under the number flaps.

Step 6: Close the anger catcher so only the numbers show.

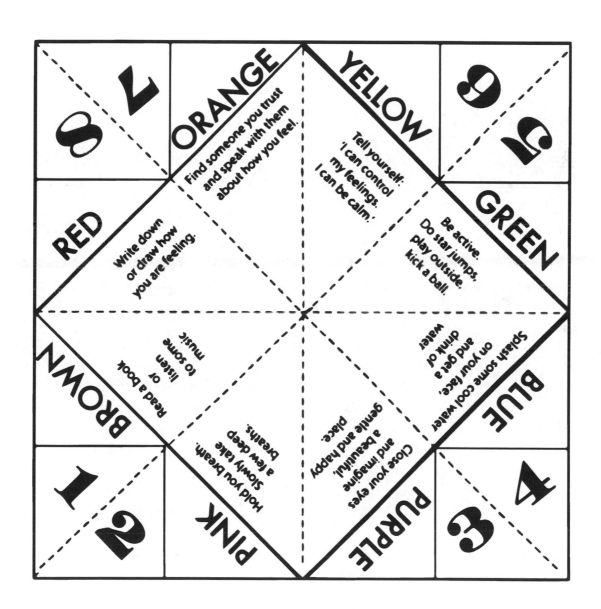

R. Ruth

Ruth 1:1-18

Today we're working with the letter ***R***

I wonder if any of you can tell me what reliable means? *(Remember to work with their answers: it is being consistent, able to be trusted).*

Being reliable means that when someone asks us to do something, they know we will be able to do it. Being reliable means that when someone needs others to turn to for help, support or a friend, then we will be there for them.

In the Book of *Ruth* we there is someone who was reliable.

Let's have a listen to what happened...

Once upon a time in the days when the judges ruled, there was a famine in the land. A man from Bethlehem named Elimelech went to live in the country of Moab, with his wife Naomi and two sons Mahlon and Chilion.

While there Elimelech died, and Naomi was left with her two sons. Her sons eventually married Moabite wives; the name of the one was Orpah and the name of the other Ruth. When they had lived there about ten years, both Mahlon and Chilion also died, so that Naomi was left without her two sons and her husband.

Naomi heard the famine had ended and there was lots of food in Bethlehem. She set out from the place where she had been living, she and her two daughters-in-law, but Naomi said to her two daughters-in-law, "Go back each of you to your mother's house. May the Lord deal kindly with you, as you have dealt with the dead and with me. The Lord grant that you may find security, each of you in the house of your husband." Then she kissed them, and they wept aloud. They said to her, "No, we will return with you to your people." But Naomi said, "Turn back, my daughters, why will you go with me? Do I still have sons in my womb that they may become your husbands? Turn back, my daughters, go your way, for I am too old to have a husband. Even if I thought there was hope for me, even if I should have a husband tonight and bear sons, would you then wait until they were grown? Would you then refrain from marrying? No, my daughters, it has been far more bitter for me than for you, because the hand of the Lord has turned against me." Then they wept aloud again. Orpah kissed her mother-in-law, but Ruth clung to her.

So Naomi said, "See, your sister-in-law has gone back to her people and to her gods; return after your sister-in-law." But Ruth said,

"Do not press me to leave you or to turn back from following you! Where you go, I will go; where you lodge, I will lodge; your people shall be my people, and your God my God. Where you die, I will die that is where I will be buried.

May the Lord do thus and so to me, and more as well, if even death parts me from you!"

When Naomi saw that she was determined to go with her, she said no more to her.

Craft Activity: Paper Chair.

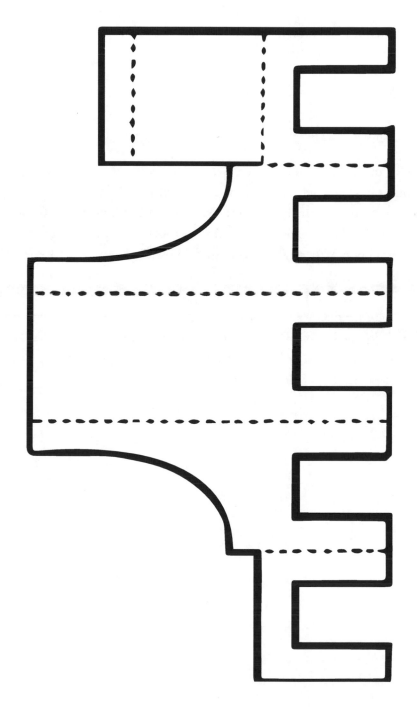

S. Sirach

Sirach 4:20-31

Today we're working with the letter *S*

I wonder if any of you can tell me what sincerity means? *(Remember to work with their answers: it is the absence of pretence, deceit, or hypocrisy).*

Sincerity is a mix of seriousness and honesty. If you do things with sincerity people will trust you because you will be serious, kind, truthful and reliable.

In the Wisdom of *Sirach* we there is someone who wrote about being sincere.

Let's have a listen to what happened...

Here is some advice on sincerity and justice. Watch for the right time; fear what is evil; do not bring shame upon yourself. There is a shame heavy with guilt, and also a shame that brings glory and respect. Show no favouritism to your own discredit; let no one intimidate you to your own downfall. Do not hold off from speaking at the proper time, and do not hide your wisdom; for wisdom becomes known through speech, and knowledge through the tongue's response. Never speak against the truth, but be ashamed of your own ignorance. Do not be ashamed to acknowledge when you fall short, and do not struggle against a rushing stream. Do not abase yourself before a fool; do not refuse to do so before rulers. Even to the death, fight for what is right, and God will do battle for you. Do not be haughty in your speech, or lazy and slack in your deeds. Do not be like a lion at home, or sly and suspicious with your servants. Do not let your hand be open to receive, but clenched when it is time to give.

T. Tobit

The Book of Tobit

Today we're working with the letter *T*.

I wonder if any of you can tell me what tearful means? *(Remember to work with their answers: sad or emotional.)*.

Being tearful can happen to any of us. When we have to say goodbye to people or things we care about. It is healthy to let these tears out but remember to let them out in a way that doesn't hurt you or others, or damage or break anything. Even if you don't seem to care now you will later on. If you're sad, remember the good times and know things will, one day be better.

In the Book of *Tobit* we are given examples of people feeling tearful.

Let's have a listen to what happened...

Once, a long time ago there lived a man named Tobit. Tobit was a righteous Israelite of the tribe of Naphtali but he, his wife and son, Tobias, lived in Nineveh. One night, this fell asleep under a tree, and while he was sleeping a bird on a branch in the tree above his poo-ed. The bird poo, which fell into his eyes, blinded him. The blindness caused by this injury made his wife want to leave him and, ultimately, he prayed for death. Meanwhile, in faraway Media, a young woman named Sarah was also praying in despair, for death. The demon, Asmodeus would abduct and kill every man Sarah married on the wedding night. God heard both their prayers but knew they would rather be happy again than dead, so God sent the angel Raphael, disguised as a human, to heal Tobit and free Sarah from the demon.Tobit, feeling that his life was over remembered a large amount of money he had deposited in the distant land of Media and sent Tobias to collect the money. Raphael, the angel in disguise, presented himself as Tobit's kinsman, Azariah, and offered to aid and protect Tobias on the journey. Under Raphael's guidance, Tobias travelled to Media with his dog. Along the way, while washing his feet in the river Tigris a fish tried to swallow his foot. By the angel's order, Tobies captured it and removed its heart, liver and gall bladder. Upon arriving in Media, Raphael told Tobias of the beautiful Sarah, whom Tobias had the right to marry because he was her cousin and closest relative. The angel instructed Tobit to burn the fish's liver and heart to drive away the demon when he attacks on the wedding night. Sarah and Tobit got married, and when Asmodeus showed up to kill Tobit, the fumes of the burning organs drove the demon to Upper Egypt, where Raphael followed and bound him. Meanwhile Sarah's father had been digging a grave to secretly bury Tobias under the assumption that he would be killed. He was surprised however to find Tobias alive and well, and so while Raphael went to recover Tobit's money Sarah's father ordered a double-length wedding feast and secretly refilled the grave. After the feast, Tobias and Sarah returned to Nineveh. There, Raphael told Tobit how to use the fish's gall to cure his father's blindness. After this Raphael told Tobias who he really was and returned to heaven.

Craft Activity: Clown/party hat.

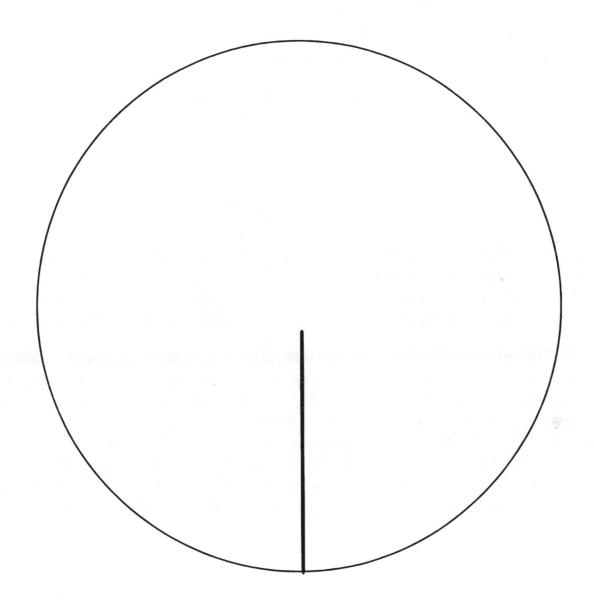

W. Wisdom

The Book of Wisdom 6:12- 7:14

Today we're working with the letter **W**.

I wonder if any of you can tell me what wise means? *(Remember to work with their answers: having or showing experience, knowledge, and good judgement).*

Being wise is something any of us can be. Being wise is to have the ability to make sound judgments and choices based on experience but also to be able to embrace nuance and multiple perspectives.

In the Book of *Wisdom* we can see how important seeking to be wise is.

Let's have a listen to what happened...

Wisdom is splendid and unfading, and she is readily seen by those who love her, and is found by those who seek her. She hastens to make herself known to those who desire her; one who watches for her at dawn will not be disappointed, for she will be found sitting at the gate. For setting your heart on her is the perfection of prudence, and whoever keeps vigil for her is quickly free from care.

I preferred her to scepter and throne and deemed riches nothing in comparison with her, nor did I liken any priceless gem to her; because all gold, in view of her, is a bit of sand, and before her, silver is to be accounted mire. I loved her beyond health and beauty, and I chose to have her rather than the light, because her radiance never ceases. Yet all good things together came to me with her, and countless riches at her hands; I rejoiced in them all, because Wisdom is their leader, though I had not known that she is their mother. Sincerely I learned about her, and ungrudgingly do I share— her riches I do not hide away. She is an unfailing treasure; those who gain this treasure win the friendship of God, being commended by the gifts that come from her discipline.

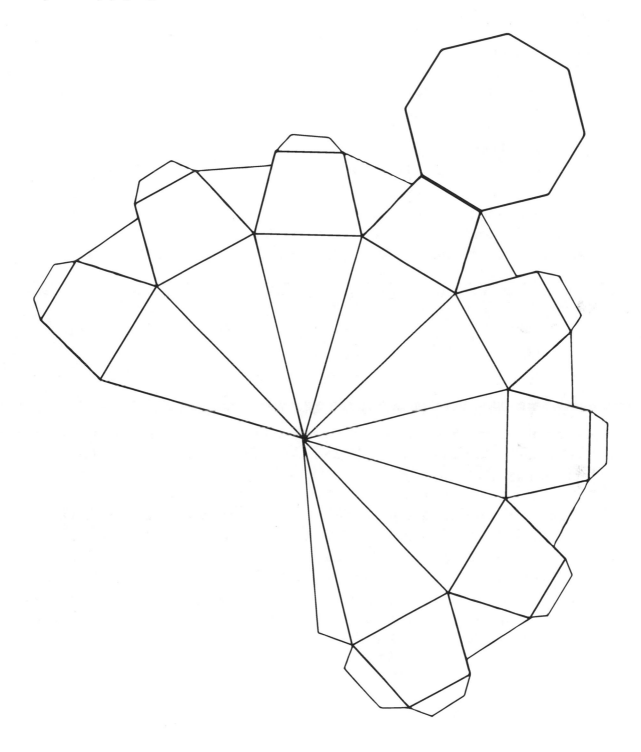

Z. The Book of Zechariah

The Book of Zechariah 14:1-5

Today we're working with the letter **Z**.

I wonder if any of you can tell me what zero means? *(Remember to work with their answers: feeling cold, or nothingness).*

Sometimes we feel like zero. Sometimes we feel like nothing. Sometimes we feel that we can get nothing right, do nothing right. But that is not true. Everyone has times in their life when they feel demotivated, lost and unhappy, when they don't know how to get out of it. Life may keep piling it on. Even when things are going wrong, they will get better. Even when we go through terrible times, things will get better. Even when we go through terrible hurts we will feel better. One way to fix this sad feeling is to do something positive.

In the Book of *Zechariah* we can see how even when terrible things happen they will get better even if we don't think they will.

Let's have a listen to what happened...

A day is coming for God, says Zechariah, when the spoils taken from you will be divided in your midst. And I will gather all the nations against Jerusalem for battle: In this terrible battle Jerusalem will lose, the city will be taken by others, houses will be robbed and plundered, women will get hurt and abused; half the city will leave and go away into exile, but the rest of the people will not be removed from the city.

Then God will go forth and fight against those nations, fighting as on a day of battle. On that day God's feet will stand on the Mount of Olives, which is opposite Jerusalem to the east. The Mount of Olives will be split in two from east to west by a very deep valley, and half of the mountain will move to the north and half of it to the south. You will flee by the valley between the mountains, for the valley between the mountains will reach to Azal. Therefore you will flee as you fled because of the earthquake in the days of Uzziah, a king of Judah. Then God, my God, will come, and all his holy ones with him and you will be safe again.

Craft Activity: Self-esteem die. Colour in and cut out the die (that's what one dice is called. Fold all lines and then stick the six messages onto each side. Then glue the black tabs to make a box. Roll and answer the questions with a positive response whenever you feel low.

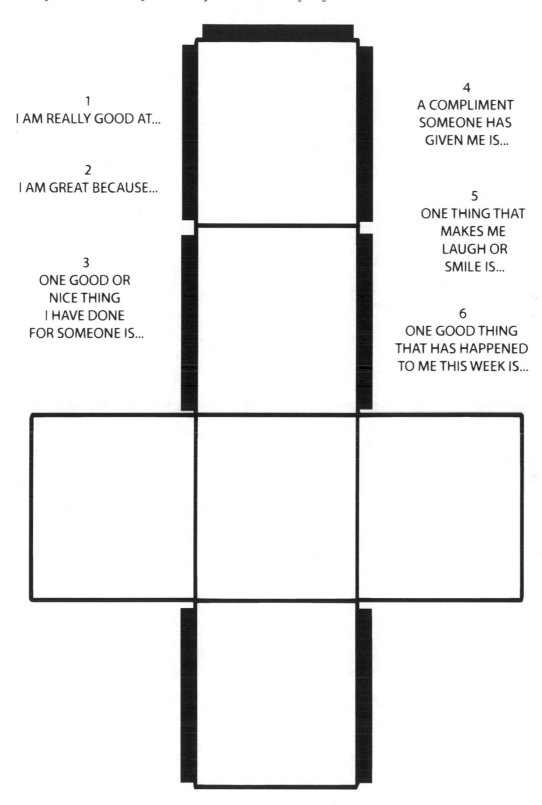

1
I AM REALLY GOOD AT...

2
I AM GREAT BECAUSE...

3
ONE GOOD OR
NICE THING
I HAVE DONE
FOR SOMEONE IS...

4
A COMPLIMENT
SOMEONE HAS
GIVEN ME IS...

5
ONE THING THAT
MAKES ME
LAUGH OR
SMILE IS...

6
ONE GOOD THING
THAT HAS HAPPENED
TO ME THIS WEEK IS...

Printed in the United States
By Bookmasters